Tackling Tumblr

Tackling Tumblr —
Web Publishing
Made Simple

Thord Daniel Hedengren

WILEY

A John Wiley and Sons, Ltd, Publication

Tackling Tumblr — Web Publishing Made Simple

This edition first published 2011

© 2011 John Wiley & Sons, Ltd

Registered office

John Wiley & Sons Ltd, The Atrium, Southern Gate, Chichester, West Sussex, PO19 8SQ, United Kingdom

For details of our global editorial offices, for customer services and for information about how to apply for permission to reuse the copyright material in this book, please see our Web site at www.wiley.com.

978-1-119-95015-8

A catalogue record for this book is available from the British Library.

Set in 10/12.5 Chapparal Pro Light by Wiley Composition Services

Printed in the United States of America by CJ Krehbiel Company

About the Author

Thord Daniel Hedengren is addicted to words. He has written two web publishing books prior to this one: *Smashing WordPress* (now in its second edition) and *Smashing WordPress Themes*, both covering WordPress. Thord runs a web agency called Odd Alice in Stockholm, Sweden, and is a frequent freelancer and occasional editor for various publishing houses. He still thinks content is king, which either makes him an utter moron or just proves his genius. Online you'll often find him under the moniker TDH. You can catch all his antics through `http://tdh.me`, where you'll also find the necessary means to stalk him across the social web. Don't worry, he likes that stuff.

Dedication

This book is dedicated to all of you who are using the Web to publish your content. Your words, your thoughts, and your opinions are just as important as the next guy's. We live in a wonderful time when everyone can be heard, so use your voice and speak your mind. It is imperative.

Publisher's Acknowledgments

Some of the people who helped bring this book to market include the following:

Editorial and Production:

VP Consumer and Technology Publishing Director: Michelle Leete
Associate Director- Book Content Management: Martin Tribe
Associate Publisher: Chris Webb
Publishing Assistant: Ellie Scott
Development Editor: Sara Shlaer
Technical Editor: Jon Phillips
Copy Editor: Maryann Steinhart
Editorial Manager: Jodi Jensen
Senior Project Editor: Sara Shlaer
Editorial Assistant: Leslie Saxman

Marketing:

Associate Marketing Director: Louise Breinholt
Marketing Executive: Kate Parrett

Composition Services:

Compositor: Wiley Composition Services
Proofreader: Susan Hobbs
Indexer: Potomac Indexing, LLC

Contents

Part I: Introducing Tumblr

CHAPTER 1
This Is Tumblr

CHAPTER 2
Getting Started with Tumblr

Introduction

THERE IS SOMETHING special about publishing online using a hosted service like Tumblr, the topic of this book. Today you have so many options when it comes to getting your message out there that it might be hard to pick the right one, but some avenues are definitely better choices than others.

Tumblr is a great choice for a publishing platform, and one of the more interesting publishing solutions as well. Contrary to popular belief, Tumblr is not solely for traditional blogging. You can use the strengths of the platform for so much more.

Despite having a low entrance barrier and being so simple to work with, Tumblr offers tremendous possibilities. In a way, Tumblr is to online publishing what the compact camera was for photography: just point and shoot and there you go — published!

I love that. And I bet you will too.

This book will teach you all you need to get started publishing on Tumblr, from signing up to creating all types of posts. You'll learn how to tie into the Tumblr community and how to link your Tumblr site to other social networks. The book goes beyond the basics, showing you how to use Tumblr for non-blogging purposes such as marketing or small business sites. And if you have some basic knowledge of HTML and CSS (or are willing to learn a bit about them), you can learn how to edit existing Tumblr themes and create new ones.

Tackling Tumblr is divided into four parts.

Part I: Introducing Tumblr

In the first part of the book you'll learn what Tumblr is and how you can use it. You'll set up your first Tumblr site, post your first few posts, and learn about the various types of posts and how to pick the right theme.

Part II: Connecting with Tumblr

Tumblr is so much more than just publishing content. In Part II you'll learn about the Tumblr community and its offerings. You'll also take a look at how you can spread the word to other social networks such as Facebook and Twitter.

Part III: Advanced Tumbling

Part III kicks it up a notch with more advanced features, such as adding comments to Tumblr sites. You'll also take a more in-depth look at how you can use Tumblr "beyond blogging."

Part IV: Tumblr Theming

In Part IV you'll learn more about Tumblr themes, from how to edit existing themes to actually building a brand new one from scratch. If you know a bit of HTML and CSS, you'll be modifying or perhaps even creating your own theme after finishing the last chapters of the book.

Keep in Touch

I can't wait to see what you'll create with Tumblr. In fact, why don't you tell me? You can find me on these fine sites and social networks:

- `http://tdhftw.tumblr.com` — My less-than-serious Tumblr blog
- `http://twitter.com/tdhedengren` — Follow and tweet me on Twitter
- `http://fb.com/tdhftw` — Keep up with my writing from my Facebook fan page
- `http://tdh.me` — I have a regular website as well

Top these off by keeping an eye on `http://tackling.tumblr.com`, where the Tackling theme lives and breathes. I'd like to hear from users of the theme, so don't be shy, get in touch.

part I

Introducing Tumblr

This Is Tumblr

THIS CHAPTER SERVES as both a quick introduction to Tumblr and an inspiration for what you can do with it. Tumblr's not all posting pictures of bacon (a popular meme) and looking at funny GIF images after all. No, there's a lot more to it, and while we'll tackle the specifics in-depth later in the book, this introduction will get your mind started on the possibilities.

What Is Tumblr?

Tumblr is a hybrid service—part blogging, part microblogging, and a social network to boot. Not a very definite description, is it? The thing with Tumblr is that it really becomes what you make of it. It's not just about understanding how the Tumblr service works, but also how you can use it for your own needs.

Blogging

Tumblr is a great blogging platform. It's easy to publish posts, there are great mobile apps for your tumbling on the go, and you've got a living theme ecosystem that offers multiple options to make your site look good. Just take a look at the Tumblr Staff blog, shown in Figure 1-1, to get an idea of the diversity of available styles and possibilities. The practice of blogging has changed dramatically during its relatively short lifespan; thanks in part to Tumblr and its cohorts you can easily publish not only blog posts but also videos, quotes, audio files, and so on. Add to that the rise of social networks like Twitter and Facebook, and you have a whole new beast.

Microblogging

Microblogging is the term used to describe the various sorts of short text publishing, usually no more than 140 characters long. It is mostly used for sharing short thoughts, links, and such, but also for social interaction. Twitter (`http://twitter.com`) is by far the most well-known microblogging service, and lets you post status updates through apps, the website, as well as using text messages.

Today microblogging is short blogging. Tumblr isn't a traditional microblogging service, but there is nothing that says that you can't use it for short status messages. This is particularly true for smartphone users that rely on the Tumblr app, because that makes it just as easy to share content through your Tumblr blog as it is to send a tweet.

FIGURE 1-1: What better way to showcase a Tumblr blog than the Tumblr Staff blog at http://staff.tumblr.com

Networking

Tumblr is also a social network, with its own memes and trends. On Tumblr you follow people much like you do on Twitter, and you can repost (or *reblog*) content to your own tumblogs. If that isn't enough, you can also "like" content on other people's tumblogs and by doing so improve their ranking within the Tumblr social network. The Tumblr network is quite immense, and if you're just getting started you might want to take a look at the Explore page, found at http://www.tumblr.com/explore (and shown in Figure 1-2).

There are two ways a Tumblr user connects to content on other Tumblr blogs: likes and reblogs. A *like* is a way of showing you like the post, symbolized by a heart, similar to the way you show supp for a posting on Facebook. *Reblogging* is actually reposting a post, or parts of it, on your own Tumblr site, with a link back of course.

NOTE

FIGURE 1-2: Explore the Tumblr community at http://www.tumblr.com/explore

A Bit of Tumblr History

Tumblr was founded in 2007 by Scott Karp, with Marco Arment as the lead developer, and the company is backed by several investors. Scott Karp is still with Tumblr, while Arment has moved on to work with the excellent bookmarking service Instapaper.com.

Over the years, Tumblr has seen massive growth. As of late early May 2011 it clocks in at more than 18 million blogs and an insane number of posts, growing higher every minute. While official figures on actual users are hard to come by, you can watch the usage ticker at `http://www.tumblr.com/about` (see Figure 1-3).

There's no doubt that Tumblr fills some sort of need in the publishing sphere. Maybe it's because it is so easy to publish using Tumblr, or maybe it is the different types of posts. It could also be the fact that the Tumblr team is really careful to avoid releasing ugly themes through the official channels (although you can download or buy themes from other sources, as well as make your own), which ensures that most tumblogs feature good design. Tumblr has come a long way since its launch only four short years ago, and is definitely here to stay.

FIGURE 1-3: Check out Tumblr growth at its website

What Can I Do with Tumblr?

Tumblr is a truly useful platform, there is no doubt about it. The tools it offers, from different kinds of posts to networking with other Tumblr users, makes it versatile and powerful. Chances are that whatever you're doing using other tools like WordPress or other blogging systems is also possible on Tumblr. Of course, that doesn't mean you should move every online project to Tumblr. Every platform has strengths and weaknesses, and you should always consider the specific needs of your project, but Tumblr is often a good choice.

You have seven different types of posts, sometimes referred to as *post types* or *post formats*, at your disposal for your Tumblr site. The post types are Text, Photo, Quote, Link, Chat, Audio and Video.

NOTE

Let's start by looking at some ways you can use Tumblr for publishing. The following sample is by no means a complete list, just a little something to show how flexible it is.

Personal Blogs

Using Tumblr to power a personal blog or journal is a no-brainer. Tumblr truly excels here; it's a great choice for a publishing platform thanks to the user-friendly interface and the various publishing apps available. If you want to write for your friends and family, or just write because you enjoy it, then Tumblr is an excellent choice. You'll be up and running in minutes, and then you can build from there.

It gets even better thanks to the post formats, which let you easily post different kinds of content. The huge number of great looking themes makes it even nicer to use Tumblr to power your blog. Figure 1-4 shows a typical personal blog.

FIGURE 1-4: All the elements of a typical personal blog — photo, text, captions, and links

Portfolios

Here's another no-brainer. Let's say you're a photographer, aspiring amateur or professional, and you want to showcase your work. Tumblr makes it easy to post photos, and you can choose from among several themes that were created to focus on visual content.

The same goes for most other artistic branches, from web designers posting screenshots of and links to their work to video producers showcasing their latest commercials, not to mention artists (see Figure 1-5). Tumblr is truly visual, and if you're in need of a portfolio showing off your work you should definitely consider using Tumblr. It gets even better because you can get nice traction and exposure within the Tumblr network thanks to likes and reblogs.

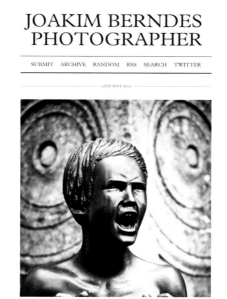

FIGURE 1-5: Joakim Berndes Phtographer (http://jberndes.tumblr.com/) works with images

Brand or Product Sites

There's nothing stopping you from using Tumblr to power a brand or product website (see Figure 1-6). In fact, Tumblr can help people share your content through reblogging and likes to further promote your brand or product. You will most likely want to create your own theme for such a website, since it needs to carry the branding itself, but you have to do that no matter what solution you use.

You get Tumblr's ease of use, as well as the connection to the Tumblr users and network. If your product or brand website relies on updates, I'd say Tumblr is a great choice. However, if you envision a static website then Tumblr's strengths won't really come into play and you might be better off using a different solution.

FIGURE 1-6: Oscar de la Renta's PR Girl website (http://oscarprgirl.tumblr.com/) is powered by Tumblr

Company Websites

Why not use Tumblr to power your company website? Smaller companies in particular would do well to use a hosted service like Tumblr for their websites rather than relying on clunky CMS solutions some savvy salesperson got them to pay top dollar for years back. While many companies prefer to use their own domain name for a website, you don't need one to get started, and neither is a web host since Tumblr takes care of that too.

With Tumblr, anyone can publish, and it's more likely that company website will be updated if it is easy to manage. You can post a few static pages to explain what the company is up to, how to get in touch, and who the staff is, and then a content flow with news and announcements. Local businesses could use this to keep in touch with their customers, accountants could use it to post changes in the tax rules, a clothing store could publish photos of new arrivals, and so on (see Figure 1-7).

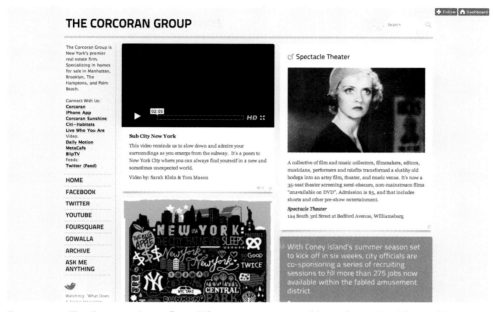

FIGURE 1-7: The Corcoran Group (http://thecorcorangroup.tumblr.com) uses Tumblr to sell homes

Podcast Presence

Publishing your podcast or video talk show usually means relying on iTunes and/or YouTube (or a similar service) to deliver each episode to your trusty listeners and viewers. However, while you should continue using those services, Tumblr adds another layer to the producer-receiver relationship. You can easily post your audio file or embed the YouTube video on Tumblr, and by doing so offer the content to the Tumblr community to like and reblog. Because it is so easy to post audio and video content on Tumblr, it's a great solution for audio and video producers wanting to keep in touch with their following and possibly gain more exposure.

If you rely solely on YouTube for viewer communication, you can interact in the comment section there, but a tumblog makes it easier to interact, and also links your brand to your production. You won't have to worry about switching providers either, so if you move from YouTube to Vimeo, for example, you will still be connected with your viewers thanks to the tumblog.

News Sites

There are numerous news sites, from conventional blog-like sites to Tumblr exposés of more traditional news outlets (see Figure 1-8). You can roll your own Engadget, Gawker, or other "blog-like but still not a blog" website using Tumblr. Better yet, you can even put ads on your news site and earn some money while you're at it. You'll probably want a custom design, but you can always get started with a free theme and then work your way up from there.

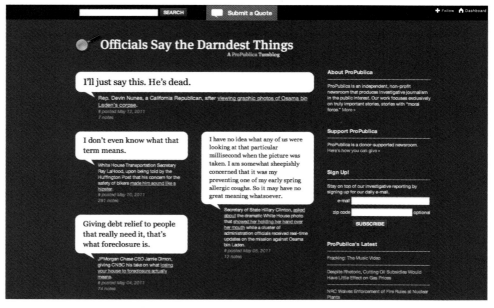

FIGURE 1-8: ProPublica.org (http://officialssay.tumblr.com/)

The Competition

Tumblr isn't the only hosted service that wants your precious words, images, and whatnot. There are numerous competing web services that let you launch free sites and provide relatively simple means for updating them. Since it is always good to know about the alternatives, here are Tumblr's main competitors.

WordPress.com

WordPress.com (Figure 1-9) is the hosted version of popular blogging platform WordPress. It's primarily a traditional blogging platform, but recent features let you run your own microblog-inspired site. The latest major update also includes Tumblr-influenced post formats, which make WordPress.com a real contender to the Tumblr service. WordPress.com is a breeze to use, but Tumblr is even easier. WordPress.com lacks the built-in social networking features that Tumblr has, such as easy reblogs and likes.

FIGURE 1-9: WordPress.com, the hosted WordPress solution

Blogger

Google's blog platform Blogger (http://blogger.com) is an oldie but still in the game. It doesn't challenge Tumblr on a feature basis as WordPress.com does, but it's still a solid solution for publishing traditional blog posts. Blogger is widespread, although I would recommend most of the other services listed here as a better option. In my book Blogger is past its prime. Figure 1-10 shows a Blogger.com site.

LiveJournal

LiveJournal (http://livejournal.com) is similar to Tumblr when it comes to the social networking aspect. Where other services from the early years of blogging continued to evolve toward simple content management systems, LiveJournal put most of its focus on the social aspect. Other than that, it is the complete opposite to Tumblr, with simple designs and close to no eye candy at all (see Figure 1-11). Unless you really want to be in the LiveJournal community, you should probably stay clear of this one.

FIGURE 1-10: J.A. Konrath's blog (http://jakonrath.blogspot.com) uses Blogger.com

FIGURE 1-11: A lot more than blogging going on at LiveJournal.com

Posterous

Perhaps the closest competitor to Tumblr is Posterous (`https://posterous.com/`), a blogging platform that truly focuses on ease of use. In fact, anyone can launch a Posterous blog just by emailing post@posterous.com. That's right, the primary idea and feature with Posterous is that you email your posts, and publish them that way. It's actually pretty cool, but other than that Posterous is a more lightweight service than Tumblr. Posterous is trying to establish some Tumblr-like social networking features but that hasn't caught on yet. Posterous is cool, but chances are Tumblr is more what you're after.

Your Own Hosted Solutions

You can always roll your own web publishing platform on your favorite webhost. This does require more technical knowledge, and you will have to worry about keeping your system up to date. The most popular alternative is, again, WordPress (`http://wordpress.org`) which also comes as a stand-alone open source alternative. Other options include Movable Type (`http://movabletype.org`) and its fork Melody (`http://melodyapp.org`); Drupal (`http://drupal.org`), which more often than not is overkill; and the Habari (`http://habariproject.org`) blog platform.

Running a site on your own install of a publishing platform is always more work than using a hosted service like Tumblr, but sometimes you need that freedom.

If you're considering using WordPress, you might be interested in my books, *Smashing WordPress: Beyond the Blog* and *Smashing WordPress Themes: Making WordPress Beautiful*. | NOTE

Summary

By now you should have a clearer picture of what Tumblr is and how you can be use it. The possibilities with the service will become even more apparent as you start playing around with a Tumblr site in Chapter 2.

chapter 2
Getting Started with Tumblr

in this chapter

- Creating a Tumblr account
- Setting up your first Tumblr site
- Getting the preferences right

IN THIS CHAPTER, you will get started with Tumblr by signing up and getting the basic settings configured. After all, you have to lay the foundation before you can start building, which in this case means you need to set everything up before you can start posting content.

After you provide the basic startup information for your Tumblr account and set your account preferences, you will learn how to set up multiple blogs. You'll also learn more about the use of domain names and how to point your tumblog to the correct domain.

Setting Up Your Tumblr Account

The first step is to sign up with Tumblr. Signing up is free and done in a breeze. This section walks you through the signup process and gives you a closer look at the account settings.

Signing Up

Getting started with Tumblr is easy. All you have to do is sign up and you're ready to go. Just type **http://www.tumblr.com** in your web browser and you'll be greeted with a nice graphic and three fields (see Figure 2-1):

- **Email address:** Enter your email address.
- **Password:** Enter a password (make sure you choose a strong password).
- **URL:** Tumblr URLs are built around subdomains of the tumblr.com domain name (you'll learn more about domain and subdomain names later in this chapter). That means that if you type **skeletor** in the URL field, you'll get skeletor.tumblr.com when registered. (Or you could, if skeletor.tumblr.com wasn't already taken.) Finding the perfect URL can be a bit of a bother. Tumblr will tell you if the URL is available when you type or click the *Start posting* button.

> **NOTE** Your URL of choice can contain only letters, numbers, and dashes. No buttons or fancy characters here, which is probably for the better since they can mess with the web browser as well.

Fill in these three fields, click *Start posting*, and voilà, Tumblr creates your first blog! The next step is to work through a few account settings.

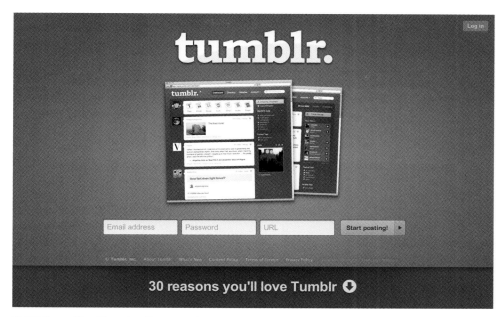

FIGURE 2-1: Tumblr makes it easy to sign up

Setting Up Tumblr

When you first sign up for a Tumblr account, you get logged in right away. The interface for publishing content, which you'll see in Chapter 3, is almost as simple, but for now, as a first-time visitor, you're greeted with the not-so-subtle graphic shown in Figure 2-2.

Close the alert by clicking the *X* button at the top right of the bubble (the *X* button only shows when you hover over the alert bubble). Tumblr now asks you to supply a blog title and upload a portrait photo (see Figure 2-3). Fill out a fancy title; I went with "TDH Testing Tumblr" since this is just a test blog for the book (you can always change the title of your tumblog later on), and browse your hard drive for a suitable avatar. Then click the big *Show all appearance options* button.

FIGURE 2-2: Tumblr really makes it easy to start posting

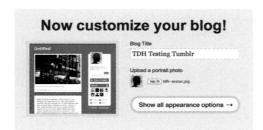

FIGURE 2-3: Blog titled and graphic selected

Next, Tumblr displays the appearance settings, with the Info tab open by default (see Figure 2-4). Notice the other tabs along the top: Themes, Appearances, Pages, Services, Community, and Advanced. I'll go into these tabs in more depth in Chapter 4, but for now just fill out a simple description for your blog on the Info tab. Leave the *Use a custom domain name* field blank for now, and click the *SAVE + CLOSE* button in the top right.

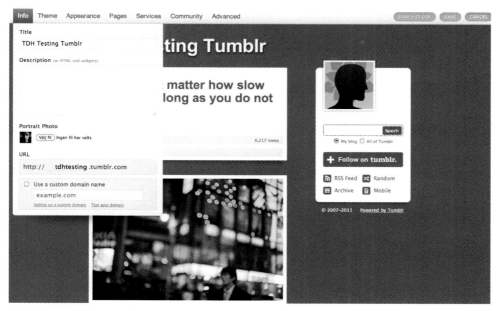

FIGURE 2-4: Fill in your blog description

> You can always go back and change your appearance settings later from your Dashboard. **NOTE**
> Just click the Customize link in the right column to return to the settings.

As you might guess, you'll be setting a lot of options and fiddling in this view when customizing your Tumblr blog, so you'll see more of it soon.

Next, Tumblr asks if you want to *follow* people (see Figure 2-5), that is, you want their posts to appear on your site. We'll get to the social networking features of Tumblr in Chapter 5, but if you like, you can find some people to follow or even look for your contacts now on Gmail, MSN, Yahoo, Hotmail, or AOL using the *Look up* feature. Play around with this screen a bit if you like, and then close the window.

FIGURE 2-5: Follow whomever you like

Finally, your Dashboard appears, as shown in Figure 2-6. On the Dashboard, you see all the Tumblr blogs you follow, much like you would see the people you follow on Twitter or friends on Facebook. By default you're just following the staff blog (`http://staff.tumblr.com`), which is pretty nice and sometimes gives some pointers. Later on you'll want to follow more blogs and get a more interesting Dashboard; we'll get to that in Chapter 5. On the right side you see some data about your Tumblr blog, including the URL, how many posts you've written, and so on.

FIGURE 2-6: The Dashboard

That's it; you're all ready to start publishing posts on your very first Tumblr blog! Next you'll take a quick peek at the account settings.

Account Preferences

It's always a good idea to check out the account settings on any online service you're using, if for no other reason than getting acquainted with them should you need to change something in the future. Tumblr is no different.

To reach your account settings, click the dropdown arrow for the *Account* menu on the top right of your Dashboard. The *Account* menu includes the *Preferences* screen, the not-too-user-friendly *Help* page, and the *Log out* link for whenever you're done tumbling. Click *Preferences* to reach your account settings page (shown in Figure 2-7).

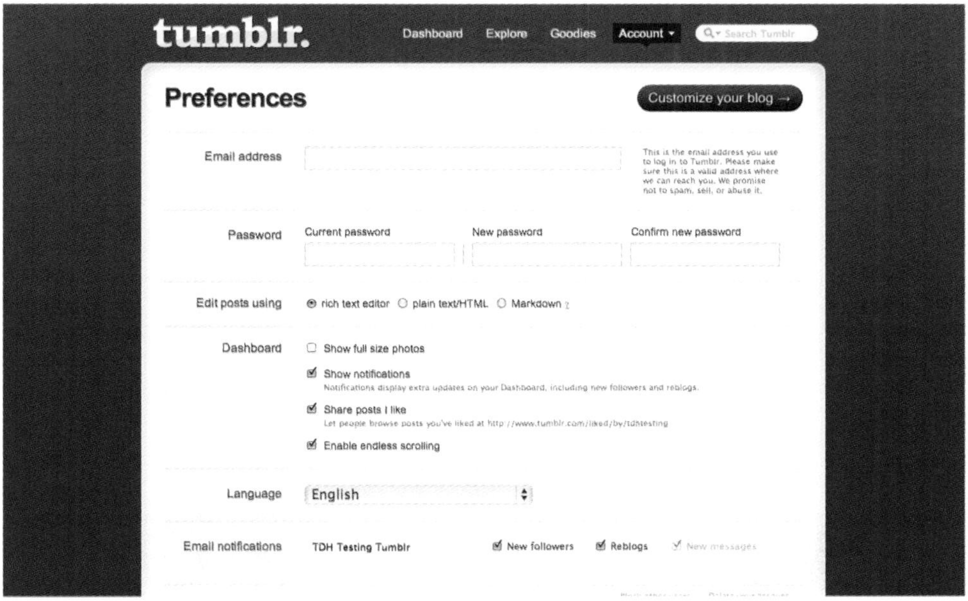

FIGURE 2-7: The Preferences page

Most of the stuff on this page is pretty self-explanatory, so here's a quick walk-through:

- The *Customize your blog* button in the top right is a quick link to the appearance view you visited earlier.
- *Email address* and *Password* should display the information you added earlier. Make sure you have a working address and a strong password in these fields. Obviously you can change these here as well as in the appearance view.

■ The *Edit posts using* setting is pretty interesting. Rich text editor is the default selection and it gives you a visual editor, much like a toned down WYSIWYG (What You See Is What You Get) view, with buttons for bold text and so on, acting much like your typical word processor. This is the best option for most people because it makes it really easy to add formatting to your posts. However, if you prefer to write the HTML yourself, select the *plain text/HTML* option. Finally, you can select the option to use *Markdown*, an alternative markup language created by John Gruber of Daring Fireball fame. You can read up on Markdown on his site (`http://daringfireball.net/projects/markdown/`) but chances are that if you intend to use it you know all about it already. I love the fact that this is an option here.

■ The Dashboard settings let you decide whether to:

- Show full-sized photos or smaller versions in the Dashboard
- Be notified of new followers and reblogs
- Make your "liked" posts page visible to people
- Enable endless scrolling, which means that if you scroll down on your Dashboard page, Tumblr will automatically add content to the bottom, rather than provide a link to older stuff

■ The language setting enables you to choose from English, German, French, and Italian (I'm sure the language options will increase as time goes by).

■ The Email notifications setting lets you decide when Tumblr should email you (when you get a message, a new follower, and a reblog).

■ Just above the *Cancel* button in the bottom right corner, you'll find links to block users and delete your account (see Figure 2-8). These links are gray so that you won't use them accidentally.

■ At the bottom of the page is a *Save preferences* button on the left, as well as a *Cancel* button on the right. Don't forget to click the former if you made any changes!

You can log out of Tumblr by selecting *Log Out* from the Account menu.

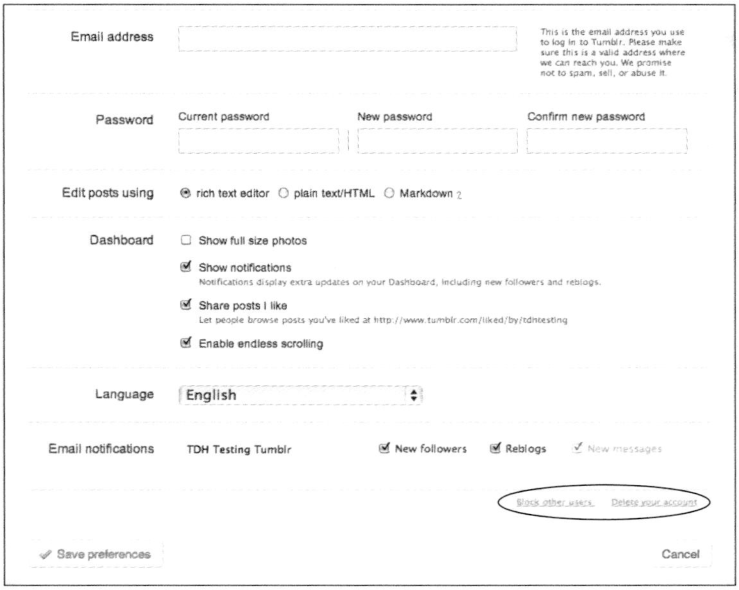

FIGURE 2-8: Use caution with these links; you can block unwanted users or delete your account.

Creating Multiple Blogs

You created your first Tumblr blog just by signing up for Tumblr. This section shows you how to create and manage multiple blogs.

If you have logged out of your account, open Tumblr and log in again. Tumblr will open to display your Dashboard. The blog name shown to the right in the Dashboard is the blog you're using right now (and the only one you have so far).

Now click the tiny down arrow beside your blog name (*TDH Testing Tumblr* in Figure 2-9) and then click the *Create a new blog* option.

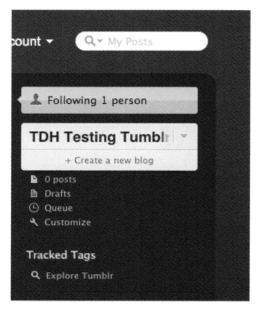

FIGURE 2-9: Just the one blog here, for now. Use the *Create a new blog* link to create a new blog.

As expected, it's easy to create a new blog. Just enter a blog title (I went with *TDH Bonus Tumblr*, as you can see in Figure 2-10), your requested URL (*tdhbonus.tumblr.com* made sense to me) and decide whether you want to password-protect your blog (I didn't). Then click *Create blog* in the bottom left and you're all set.

Create a new blog

This will create a full-featured blog with the special ability to manage multiple authors.

Title	TDH Bonus Tumblr	(ie. Acme Corp, Sara & Jacob, My Awesome Blog)
URL	tdhbonus.tumblr.com	(you can change this at any time)
Privacy	☐ Password protect this blog	
	This blog can only be viewed by people who enter this password	

✓ Create blog   Cancel

FIGURE 2-10: Creating the TDH Bonus Tumblr blog

This time you won't have to go through the whole Tumblr guide to everything; you'll just end up in your Dashboard with the newly created blog selected. Tumblr assumes that if you're creating a second blog, you already know how the system works. By default, you're not even autofollowing the staff blog here, so it's a really empty Dashboard, as you can see in Figure 2-11.

FIGURE 2-11: Not much going on for TDH Bonus Tumblr here

You can post content to your new blog as well as customize it using the Customize link on the right side. For now, the important thing is that you understand how incredibly simple it is to add additional blogs to your Tumblr account. A breeze, right?

Now swap back to the first blog again, clicking that little arrow to the right of the blog name on the right side. As you can see in Figure 2-12, the TDH Testing Tumblr blog is now selectable, along with the option of creating yet another Tumblr blog. It's as simple as that.

The blog shown to the right in the Dashboard is the one currently selected. That's important to remember, because should you click any of the posting icons at the top and add content, you are adding content to the one selected (open). You can change that on the actual post screen, as you'll see in the next chapter, but it's worth remembering to check to avoid posting content to the wrong blog.

IMPORTANT

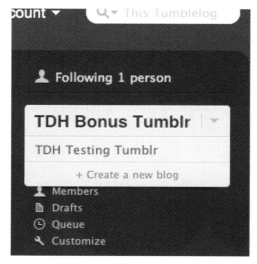

FIGURE 2-12: Pick your blog

The data under the blog obviously changes when you change the blog as well, so your drafts are stored on a per blog basis.

Using Your Own Domain or Subdomain Name

You may need to adjust one setting before you move along and start posting content. From your Dashboard, click Customize under your blog name on the right side to get to the appearance page for your blog. Then click Info in the top menu to get the dropdown with your blog details, which you'll no doubt remember from earlier in this chapter.

At the bottom of this panel you can opt to use your own domain name. To do that, you need to actually own a domain name, such as yourname.com or tdh.me. To own a domain name you need to register it with a *registrar*, a company that registers domain names for you.

> **TIP** If you want to register a domain name, you can choose from among the many available domain registrars. Most web hosts will register domain names for you, but since Tumblr is a hosted service you might not have another web host. Some registrars that you might want to check out include godaddy.com, namecheap.com and directnic.com.

You can always use a tumblr.com subdomain, and if you're happy with that you don't have to worry about this part; simply leave the checkbox for *Use a custom domain name* unchecked. However, if you want to use a custom domain, this is where you enter the settings. Figure 2-13 shows the checkbox ticked to enter a custom domain name.

FIGURE 2-13: You can choose your own domain name

Why would you want to use your own domain name? Well, for starters it is probably easier to remember than your Tumblr address. Choosing your own domain is also a way to underline your own credibility, as well as to strengthen your brand. Imagine if Microsoft didn't have microsoft.com, but instead used microsoft.tumblr.com. Having your own domain name looks good and is generally a good idea if you're presenting a business or brand, or just yourself for that matter.

Tumblr works with both top-level domains such as yourdomain.com, and subdomains, such as mytumblr.yourdomain.com. To make it work, you need to point your domain (or subdomain) to Tumblr so that Tumblr can direct users to the right place. This might be a bit tricky depending on your registrar.

To point your domain to your Tumblr site you'll need to visit your registrar. (If these instructions are beyond your technical comfort zone, don't hesitate to contact your registrar's support.) Your registrar uses various kinds of *records,* such as CNAME, MX, and A records, to route your domain all over the web. Each type of record handles a different task; for example, MX records are used primarily for mail. When you want to point your domain to Tumblr, the only thing you need to worry about is the A record.

To point your domain to Tumblr, create an A record and point it to 72.32.231.8, which is an IP address. This points your custom domain to Tumblr, allowing your visitors to simply type in your custom domain (tdhbonus.com) to find your site instead of your initial Tumblr sub-domain (tdhbonus.tumblr.com). This could take several days to take effect; how long it actually takes to point your domain depends on DNS servers all across the Internet. You should at least give it 48 hours before contacting support.

> **NOTE** Make sure that you alter only your domain's A record when pointing it to Tumblr. You don't need to change anything else, just the A record. If you're uncertain of how to do this you should consult your registrar's support.

You will know that your custom domain name is pointing to Tumblr and working correctly when you type it in the browser's address bar and it sends you to the Tumblr homepage instead of sending you a holding page provided by your registrar.

After you confirm the domain is pointing to Tumblr, go to the appearance page and fill out your domain details there. Failure to do so will send users who type in your custom domain name to the Tumblr homepage, and you want those users to be directed to your tumblog, not the Tumblr homepage.

Remember to check the *Use the custom domain name* option, and click the *SAVE + CLOSE* button when you're done. Assuming all went well, typing that same domain in your web browser's URL field will now send you to your Tumblr blog. Likewise, typing your Tumblr blog's subdomain address will send you to your custom domain, which is what you wanted. There's more on setting up custom domains at `http://www.tumblr.com/docs/en/custom_domains/`. You can also find a test tool there to see if everything is set up correctly.

Does all this sound way too complicated to you? Then just contact your registrar (where you bought your domain name) and have them point the A record to the 72.32.231.8 IP address. Then you do the necessary setting on the appearance page for your blog, and all should be fine.

> **NOTE** Don't be stressed out if your domain doesn't work right away. It takes some time for domains to point to a new destination, and sometimes it happens gradually. That means that your friends might see the old location, whereas you see the new one. Give it time — 72 hours at least — before you start complaining.

Summary

You're getting there! Now you not only have your Tumblr account set up, but you also have a Tumblr site (or several) to play with. This means that you are ready to start publishing content. That's the fun part, so in the next chapter you'll dive right into the various ways you can publish your words, photos, videos, quotes, and more using Tumblr.

chapter 3
Your First Tumblr Post

TUMBLR HAS A very intuitive interface, so if you have played around a bit you probably have an idea of how things work. This chapter will teach you how to use the various types of posts — text, photos, chat, and more. You'll also learn about the post settings and how to queue your posts. When you have finished reading this chapter you'll be more than ready to start publishing content to your Tumblr site.

The Tumblr Post Types

On Tumblr, you use *post types* to separate different kinds of content. You have seen the post types already, represented by icons in your Dashboard, as shown in Figure 3-1.

FIGURE 3-1: The post type icons on the Tumblr Dashboard

There are currently seven different post types available on Tumblr:

- **Text** posts are meant for typical text-heavy posts. The usual blog post would be a text post.
- **Photo** posts are formatted to display your images, whether photos or other formats.
- **Quote** posts are for — wait for it — quotes.
- **Link** posts are for sharing links with your readers.
- **Chat** posts are for posting a dialogue, conducted via IM or whatever, with the formatting to display it in a reasonable fashion.
- **Audio** posts are for publishing audio files for your listener's pleasure.
- **Video** posts are for sharing videos, whether it is something you found online and want to embed, or a video that you upload to Tumblr itself.

Depending on the theme you're using your posts will look different. You'll explore themes in Chapter 4, but most themes will stick to the same basic concept, meaning that no matter which theme you choose, you will always have the same post types and often each of those post types will have a slightly different design.

Post Settings

Before we go through each of the post types in detail, let's take a look at the post settings, which are the same for all post types. You'll find them on the right side of any post writing view, so click the *Text post* button to open the view. Here you can select the Tumblr blog to post to, when to publish the post, and other settings (see Figure 3-2).

FIGURE 3-2: The post settings

At the top is a simple dropdown menu that allows you to pick the Tumblr blog you want to publish to. Your original blog may appear as "my blog" or by its actual name; if you have more than one blog you'll see the titles of all your other blogs on the list. In Figure 3-2 I selected the Tackling Tumblr blog.

The next dropdown lets you specify when the post should be published:

- **publish now** is the default value; the post will go online right away.

- **queue** lets you put the post in a queue to be released later (more on that in a little bit).

- **publish on . . .** lets you set a specific date to publish the post.

- **save as draft** allows you to continue to work on the post later.

- **private** means only you will be able to see the post; this setting can be a great tool for storing notes, links and such.

The next field is the post date, which you can fill in if you selected the *publish on . . .* option in the preceding field. Here you can enter information like "tomorrow, 2am" or "3pm." There's no calendar interface; you just type when you want the post published. Tumblr understands most formats for these entries, but the various date formats used across the world can be really confusing for users. Hopefully Tumblr will improve on this system in the future.

The *content source* field is for a URL, so if you want to credit a source with your post you put the URL here. Crediting the source isn't just the right thing to do; the original content creators may complain of copyright infringement to Tumblr, which could result in Tumblr closing your account.

Tags are simple, and global so other people might find your post when browsing tag archives. It's a good idea to tag, obviously. Tags are separated by commas, so the following line would be four tags:

iPad, cloud, Elvis Presley, elsewhere

You'll see your tags displayed as small boxes, as shown in Figure 3-3 on the right.

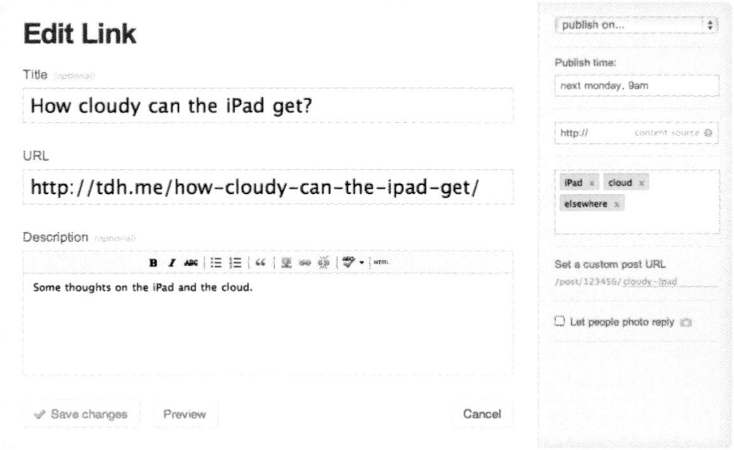

FIGURE 3-3: Notice the date settings and pretty tag graphics

Tags are all over the web these days. Basically, tags are keywords describing content, be it a text post on your Tumblr blog, or your recently uploaded photo on Flickr. Most sites let you click the tag for an archive of all content tied to that particular tag. On Tumblr, tags can be multiple words, whereas some other sites only allow tags without a space.

NOTE

In the next field, you can choose to *Set a custom post URL*. This makes the URL to your post more personal, or just plain readable. The options here are limited to the last portion of the URL. By default Tumblr will try to make a decent URL based on the title of your post, but that's not always the best way to go, and not all posts have titles.

Take a look at this post as an example: `http://tackling.tumblr.com/post/5138201293/`**`tackling-tumblr-theme`**. The bold part of the name was designated in the custom post URL field for this particular post. Had I not changed it, the URL would've been something like this: `http://tackling.tumblr.com/post/5138201293/`**`tackling-tumblr-will-feature-a-brand`**, with the bold part autocreated from the post title ("Tackling Tumblr will feature a brand new Tumblr theme"). The custom one makes a lot more sense, right? Not only that, it makes the post easier to find for people searching for the Tackling Tumblr theme using a search engine.

Finally, you have the option to let people reply to your post with a photo. Yes, that matters because Tumblr is, after all, a social network as well as a publishing platform.

The Queue

The queue feature on Tumblr is great. I wish other platforms had it as well. You can schedule posts on Tumblr, as described previously, but queuing is different. With queuing, Tumblr will spread out your posts in the queue according to your wishes. So if you tell Tumblr to spread out the posts in the queue between 9am and 7pm, it will do just that, publishing the queued posts evenly during this period. You can also decide the maximum number of posts you want to publish per day, thus spreading the queue over several days, and control the order of the posts by dragging and dropping posts.

Utilizing the queue is a great way to spread the content over several days (see Figure 3-4), making your Tumblr site a lot more interesting (and saving yourself some time). Click Queue under your site's name on the right side of your Dashboard to access the Queued Post settings.

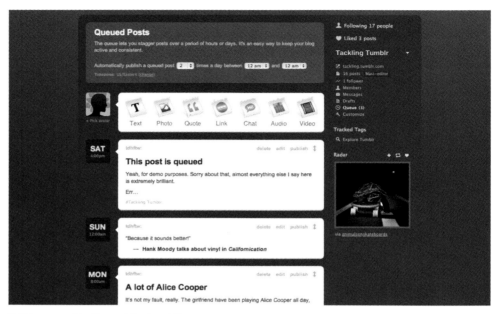

FIGURE 3-4: The Queued Posts settings

TIP If you find yourself full of inspiration, cranking out posts, quotes, and images at a fast pace is great. However, that doesn't mean that you have to, or even should, publish it all at once. By scheduling the content, either by setting a specific time and date for each post to be published, or by using the queue feature, your Tumblr site will be updated in a suitable fashion across the day. Your readers will appreciate it, and should you continue to stay ahead of the game by producing a lot of content then you can either fine-tune your publishing schedule, or work knowing that the next couple of days are covered on your site should you have to focus on something else for a while.

Writing Text Posts

Writing a text post is easy. Just click the Text post icon in your Dashboard to open the *Add a Text Post* screen (Figure 3-5).

Enter your post title in the top box, and the actual post content in the box below. That's about it. Depending on the editor settings you have (see Chapter 2), you'll see some different things in your post content box, but if you are using the visual editor you will see familiar buttons for bold, italics, and so on, as shown in Figure 3-6. To use them, either click them and just start typing, or select the text you want to make bold, for example, and click the *B* button for bold.

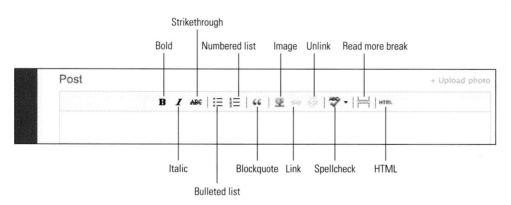

FIGURE 3-5: You can add text posts from this screen

FIGURE 3-6: The visual editor is familiar to anyone having used a word processor

From left to right, the formatting buttons for your post content are:

- **B** for bold text.
- **I** for italic text.
- **Strikethrough ABC** for strikethrough text to signal that it is deleted and/or not adequate anymore.
- **Bulleted** list.

- **Numbered** list.
- **Blockquote** for your quoting needs within the post.
- **Image** for inserting images.
- **Link** and **unlink** for adding a link or removing one.
- **Spellcheck** (ABC and a checked symbol) for spellchecking your text.
- **Read more break** if you want a read more link to get to the full content.
- **HTML** button for quick switching to HTML view.

You should definitely play around a bit to get acquainted with these buttons. Knowing your tools is always important.

An Example Text Post

The following description walks you through writing a post and shows you how to use the formatting buttons. The example is from the Tackling Tumblr site (`http://tackling.tumblr.com`), but you can follow along on your own Tumblr blog. If you haven't already done so, open Tumblr and log in if needed. If you have more than one blog, select the one you want to post to, as described in Chapter 2. From the Dashboard, click the Text icon.

The Title field at the top is optional, but most of the time you'll want a title for your post, and it is also a good idea because it gives search engines something to read and list when they're crawling your site.

For Title, I entered "The necessities when writing a book," as you can see in Figure 3-7.

FIGURE 3-7: The title's in!

Next you need some actual post content. I have prepared a short post for this, which features the necessities when writing a book (a topic that's highly individual in itself, but that really doesn't matter right now). Figure 3-8 shows how it looks completely unformatted.

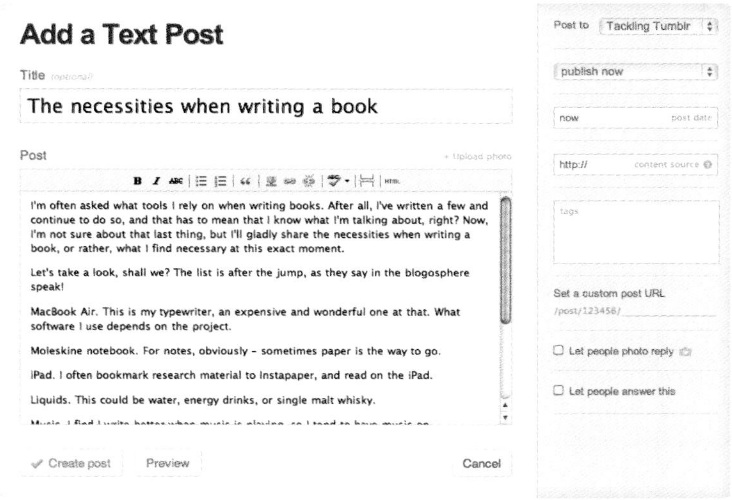

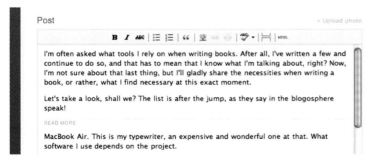

FIGURE 3-8: The content is in, unformatted

Now for the formatting. First, I don't want the full post on the front page of my Tumblr blog, so I added a *read more* link after "as they say in blogosphere speak!". I just put the cursor there, and click the *read more* icon in the editor. Clicking that icon inserts a dotted line with the grayed out text "READ MORE" where I had the cursor, as shown in Figure 3-9.

FIGURE 3-9: The *read more* link is displayed in the editor with a dotted line and the text "READ MORE"

Next, the five lines after the READ MORE link should actually be bullets in a list. There's a button for that as well, so I just select the five lines and click the *bullet list* button in the editor. Figure 3-10 shows the result. As with every formatting tool in the editor, you can just press it when writing to create the desired effect, but I had the text already written so selecting was easier.

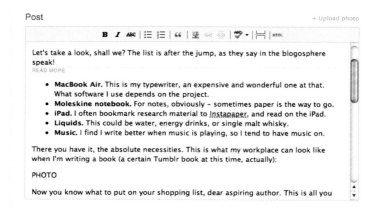

FIGURE 3-10: Bullet list

As you can also see in Figure 3-10, between the second to last and last paragraph, I've written "PHOTO" as a placeholder for where I want to place a photo that is stored on my computer.

First, I remove the "PHOTO" text and place the cursor on the empty line. Click the *Upload photo* link just above the post editor on the right side to browse your computer for a photo. The browser window will open, as shown in Figure 3-11. Pick the photo you like and click *Open*.

Now the *Upload photo* link will be replaced by a spinning graphic that indicates that the photo is being uploaded. How long that takes depends on the size of the file you're uploading and your Internet connection. It's a good idea not to upload very large images because they will just take a lot of time for the reader to load anyway.

The photo is automatically inserted into the post where your cursor was. Mine was on the blank line where "PHOTO" was before, so now I have my nice little workstation photo there, as shown in Figure 3-12.

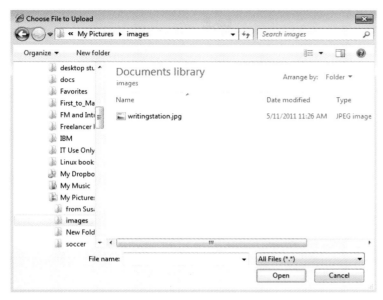

FIGURE 3-11: Upload a photo

FIGURE 3-12: The uploaded photo is now in my visual editor

You can also insert photos from elsewhere online using the *photo* icon in the post editor. Clicking that icon brings up the dialog shown in Figure 3-13, where you can specify the image URL (the address to the image you want to display), the image description, how you want the image aligned (left, right, top and so on), as well as what dimensions it should be displayed in (width and height in pixels).

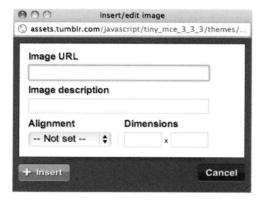

FIGURE 3-13: The image insertion settings dialog

You can also edit inserted images by clicking them in the editor (the photo will be dimmed) and then clicking the image icon. Figure 3-14 shows how it looks for my image. I added the description and set the alignment to middle, but the image URL is displayed automatically thanks to the fact that I uploaded the image to Tumblr. Clicking the *Insert* button in this case actually just updates the selected image; otherwise it would've inserted the image into the post.

Because this is a post about my necessities when writing books, I might as well take the chance to link to my book page on http://tdh.me/books/. The second sentence in the first paragraph has the words "I've written a few" (books, that is) and I think that would be great anchor text for a link. Selecting these words and then clicking the link icon in the toolbar brings up the Insert/edit link dialog. Here you set the link URL (that's where you want the link to go, http://tdh.me/books/ in this case), the link title (good for search engines trying to read your site and used as a description for the link), as well as the target which is where the link should open (this window or a new one). With the dialog filled in, as in Figure 3-15, clicking the *Insert* button adds the link to the selected words.

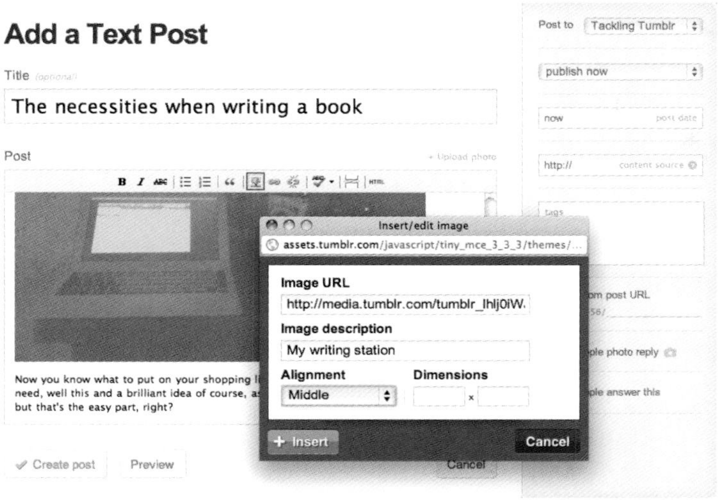

FIGURE 3-14: Using the image settings to make sure the image ends up where it should

FIGURE 3-15: Adding a link to my book page

Finally, I want to add some extra formatting to that list. The first words in each bullet should be bold; that will look good and make it easier to read. I can do this by selecting the words I want to make bold, and then clicking the B icon in the toolbar. The words are instantly in bold. Can't get much easier than that, can it?

That's it for formatting the post. Just a few more things before I hit that elusive *Create post* button in the lower left corner. Figure 3-16 shows where my post stands right now.

FIGURE 3-16: Almost there!

The only thing left is to set the post settings on the right side. At the top is the setting for what site this will be published to (Tackling Tumblr for this example, see Figure 3-16) and when the post is to be published (I want it to go online right away, so I selected *publish now*). I don't need to set a post date because I'm publishing it right now. There is no source for this content — it's all original material and there's no need to credit anyone else for it — so I'm leaving the content source field empty.

Tagging is a good idea. Tags are separated with commas, so I'll add tags for "books," "writing," and ego tag myself as "TDH" as well. Oh, and "lists," because there is a list in the post and people like lists.

So these will be converted into nice looking tags in the tags box:

books, writing, TDH, lists

In fact it happens as you type, so you can easily see what each tag looks like, in case you forgot a comma or misspelled something. The little X to the right of each tag lets you remove it with a click if you change your mind. Figure 3-17 shows the tags in the box.

The custom URL option is nice for making the URL to your post a bit prettier. I think "necessities" would look good in the URL field, so I add that. URLs are read by search engines, so it is usually a good idea to add something here.

Finally, I want to let people reply to my post using both photos and by commenting, so checkboxes for both of those options are ticked. (The "Let people answer this" option won't be available unless you have activated the replies feature which you'll find on the theme customization screen, under the Community tab. You'll learn more about replies in Chapter 7.)

That's it! Figure 3-17 shows the post, ready to be published. The *Preview* button will show me a preview of how the post will look, and then I can click the *Create post* button to publish the post to the Tackling Tumblr blog.

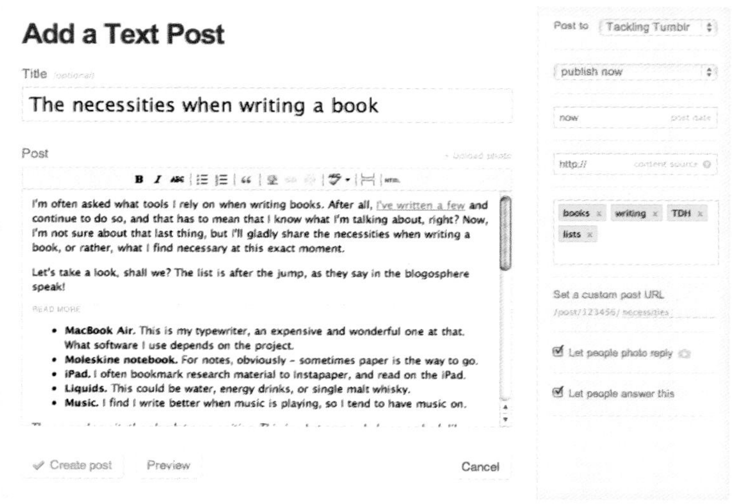

FIGURE 3-17: The post is just a click from being published

After publishing a post, Tumblr returns you to the Dashboard, where your post will be at the top, as shown in Figure 3-18. Note the READ MORE link as well as the tags, and the "Answers enabled" message below the post. There are also delete and edit links for each post.

Figure 3-19 shows the post as it appears online. You can see the example post online at `http://tackling.tumblr.com/post/3662043018/necessities`, but it will probably look different because I'll change the theme of the Tackling Tumblr blog in later chapters.

FIGURE 3-18: The Dashboard, after publishing the post

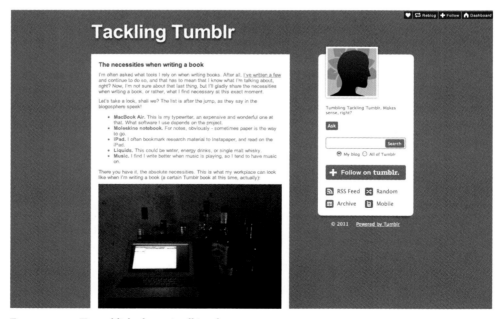

FIGURE 3-19: The published post in all its glory

Using Photo Posts

It is important to remember that Photo posts are not just for actual photos, they are for all kinds of images. Your "photo" could just as well be a drawing you did in a graphic program, or just about any image file (JPG, PNG, GIF, or BMP). Tumblr writes "photo" everywhere, but it doesn't have to be a photo. With that in mind, click Photo on your Dashboard to get to the Upload a Photo screen, shown in Figure 3-20.

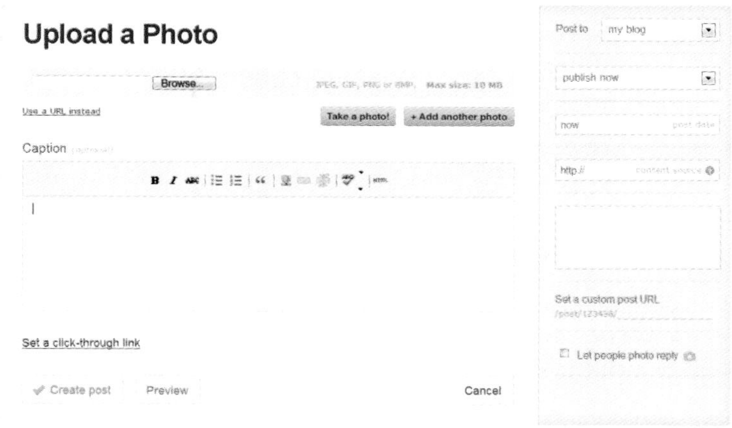

FIGURE 3-20: The Upload a Photo screen

There are three ways to post a photo (image) to your Tumblr site:

- Upload a photo to Tumblr.

- Take a photo with your webcam and directly upload it to Tumblr.

- Publish a photo from elsewhere on the Web.

You already saw how to upload a photo from your local computer in the text post example. You can use the *Browse* button at the top of the Upload a Photo screen (see Figure 3-20) the same way. Browse to select a photo, click Open, and the photo is uploaded to Tumblr. Click the *Add another photo* button under the upload area to upload, you guessed it, another photo. Figure 3-21 shows a photo post with two photos set for upload. When you have several photos you have the option to add a caption to each of them. I'm queuing this one, so the button on the bottom left doesn't say *Create post*, but rather *Queue post*. I also tagged the post and set the source to my Flickr page since that's where I snagged the photos.

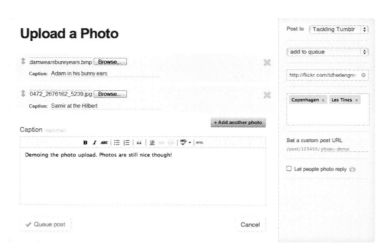

FIGURE 3-21: Uploading two photos

Again, consider the size of image files you're uploading, since it can take some time, as the upload bar in Figure 3-22 shows.

FIGURE 3-22: Uploading these photos will take some time

You can also upload a photo from your webcam. You need a webcam, of course, and Flash on your computer as well. (The web browser will urge you to download Flash if you don't have it.) Click the *Take a photo!* button and you get a big box with a *SNAP PHOTO* button, as seen in Figure 3-23. You may also see a message telling you to allow Flash to get access to the webcam.

When everything is set up, you'll see yourself (or whatever the webcam is pointing to) in the big black square shown in Figure 3-23. To take a photo with the webcam, click the big *SNAP PHOTO* button. You'll get a countdown and snap — there's your photo (Figure 3-24 is me not wanting to participate)! And yes, it gets mirrored; that's the way it works.

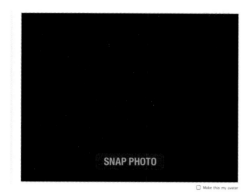

FIGURE 3-23: You might have to give Flash access to the webcam to use the Take a photo feature

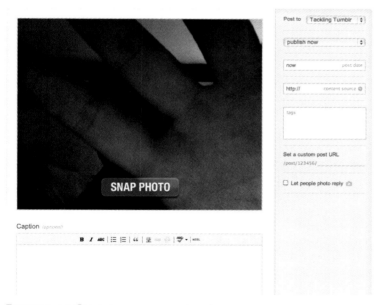

FIGURE 3-24: Get away, you paparazzi you!

The third way to add a photo is by supplying a URL. On the Upload a Photo screen, click the *Use a URL instead* link located just below the upload box. Instead of uploading or snapping a photo, you'll get a photo URL box where you can paste the URL to a photo. In Figure 3-25, I've posted the URL to the cover of one of my books because I'm all about self-marketing. I also added a caption to the image, since it might need some explaining.

FIGURE 3-25: Adding an image via URL

Before posting this image, I want to set a click-through link, which is where the reader will end up when he clicks the photo. Clicking the *Set a click-through link* link just above the *Create post* button gives me a box where I can paste a URL to which a click on the photo will lead. My page for said book would make sense, don't you think? Figure 3-26 shows the dialog just before I published this post.

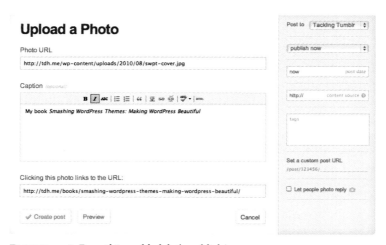

FIGURE 3-26: Everything added, let's publish!

The result? Check out Figure 3-27, which features the photo linked to the page for the book on my site.

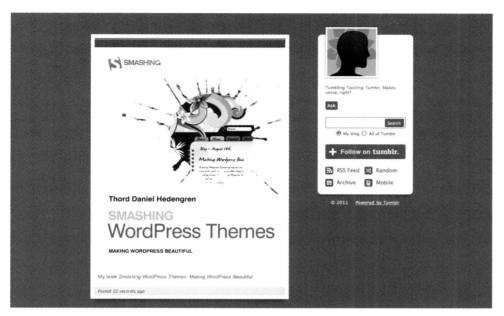

FIGURE 3-27: The published post

While you can easily use any image online thanks to the URL linking process , that doesn't mean you should. Make sure the images you are using are licensed appropriately for reuse. This is obviously not a problem for your own images, and there are quite a lot of images available for use under the Creative Commons license: http://creativecommons.org. Overall, the rule is to not steal other people's work, and to credit images that you are allowed to republish.

Keep in mind that not all image sources are fine with you just including the URL to their image, in effect loading it from their server. That could result in complaints to Tumblr, which could lead to you having your account closed down. If you link images this way, make sure you do it from sources that allow embedded use, such as Flickr for example, and that the images you select are not labeled as "All rights reserved."

Quote It with Quote Posts

Posting quotes is a nice way to lighten up almost any site, and Tumblr makes it easy to add them. From your Dashboard, click the Quote icon to reach the Add a Quote screen. This one is really straightforward, with a Quote box at top, and then the Source box, which is optional (but highly recommended), below. There is no styling for the quote itself, but you can style the source if you like, much like you do when styling text in the text posts.

That's all there is to it! Figure 3-28 shows a quote, ready to be published. It is that easy.

FIGURE 3-28: A nice little quote

Link It with Link Posts

Link posts can be very useful for the visitor to your blog. Like quote posts, the link posts are really straightforward when it comes to publishing. From the Dashboard, click Link to reach the Add a Link screen. Fill in the Title field with text that you want to appear as the clickable link, and add the URL in the second field.

If you like you can add a description to your link. Just click the Add a description link to show the now familiar visual editor box with the toolbar for easy formatting and everything. Figure 3-29 shows a somewhat egotistical link post to the Tackling Tumblr site.

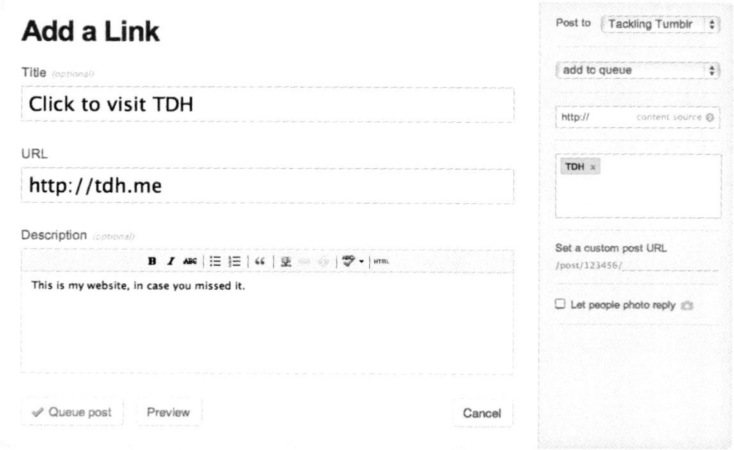

FIGURE 3-29: A link post ready to go

Figure 3-30 shows the resulting post.

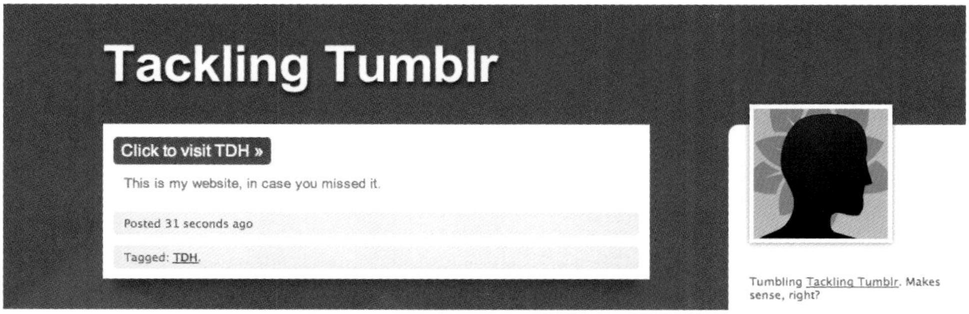

FIGURE 3-30: A published link post, ready to send visitors my way

Talk It Out with Chat Posts

Chat posts are pretty interesting. At first you might have a hard time figuring out when they are even remotely useful, but then someone hits you up on MSN (or another IM application) and you have a hilarious exchange that you just have to share with the world, like the one depicted in Figure 3-31. You reach the Chat screen via the corresponding icon in your Dashboard, as always.

FIGURE 3-31: An interesting conversation

There aren't many settings on this screen. The title is optional, and then comes the dialog, with no formatting or anything. In the dialog box you put each separate comment from each speaker on its own row, so it's pretty straightforward. Tumblr, using your theme, will then format the dialog to something a lot easier to read. Figure 3-32 shows the exchange from Figure 3-31 as it looks when published.

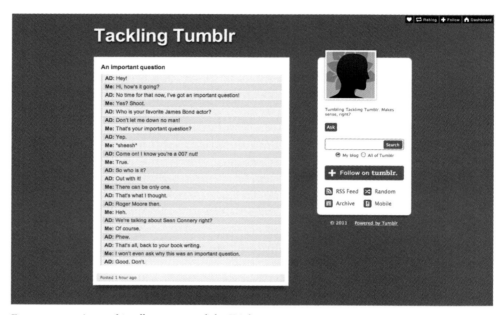

FIGURE 3-32: A user-friendly way to read the IM discussion

Audio Posting

Tumblr also supports audio files. From the Dashboard, click the Audio icon to reach the Upload an Audio Post screen (shown in Figure 3-33). Here you can either upload an audio file from your local machine, or use an audio file from someplace else online by clicking the *Use an externally hosted audio file* link below the audio file browser, and then pasting the audio file URL there.

FIGURE 3-33: The Upload an Audio Post screen

There are some rules for audio files on Tumblr, stated in the top right. They are:

- You can upload one audio file each day.
- MP3s only.
- 10 MB maximum.

This can be quite limiting, although an MP3 file that is 10 MB can be pretty long.

If you choose to link to an external file, you should know that the file will be streamed from that location. That means that whoever is hosting said audio file will be paying the Internet traffic bill, so make sure you're allowed to leech on it.

Other than that, the audio posts are much like most other post types on Tumblr, with an optional description where you can format the text. This is a piece of cake for you by now, right?

MP3 is a compressed audio format used in most digital music players, on computers and so on. Depending on how tightly it is compressed, when created the sound will be more or less crisp and close to the original. The more tightly you compress the MP3 file, the smaller it will be, but the sound quality will be reduced. There are numerous tools that can create MP3 files, and if you're recording yourself chances are you can export your work to MP3.

NOTE

Posting Video Posts

It is always fun to show video, and naturally Tumblr supports video posts as well. From the Dashboard, click the Video icon to reach the Add a Video screen, shown in Figure 3-34. From here you can either embed videos from other services such as YouTube, Blip, or Vimeo, or you can upload a video to Tumblr. As with audio files, there are some limits to what you can do if you choose to upload your video to Tumblr:

■ Each file can be at most 100 MB in size.

■ You can upload a total of 5 minutes of video per day.

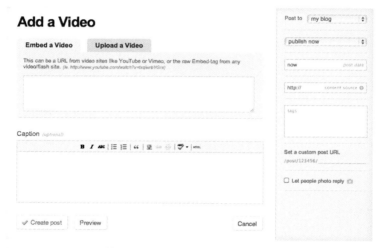

FIGURE 3-34: The Add a Video screen

Given these limitations, chances are you prefer to use services such as YouTube or Vimeo. These services put fewer limitations on your videos in terms of length and file size, and since Tumblr supports embedding you might as well use them. Some of the video sharing sites, such as YouTube and Vimeo, support a feature called oEmbed. With oEmbed, you don't have to find the embed code to embed the video on Tumblr; you can just paste the link to the video in the Embed a Video field and Tumblr will automagically embed the video in your post. In Figure 3-35, I have embedded an excellent music video from YouTube just by pasting the URL to the YouTube page.

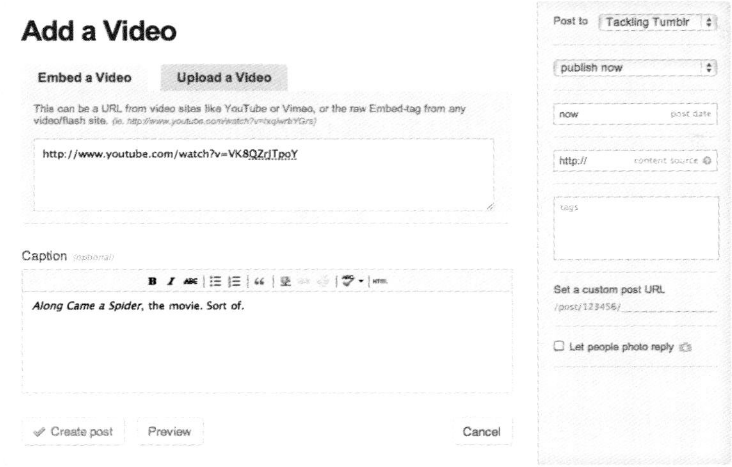

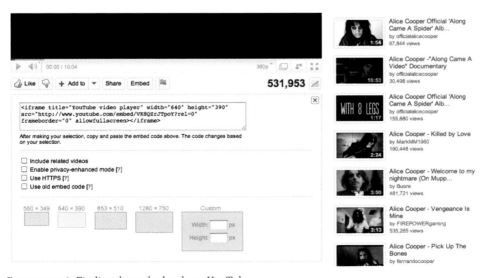

FIGURE 3-35: Embedding with just the URL

I could just as well have pasted the embed code found on the YouTube page (see Figure 3-36, showing the embed code dialog found via the Embed button) but it just isn't necessary for this one. Other than that, video posts works the same as most other posts, so just publish away.

FIGURE 3-36: Finding the embed code on YouTube

Most video file formats are supported; Tumblr is nice that way.

Summary

This chapter taught you all you really need to know to start publishing posts on your Tumblr site. The best way to grow accustomed to the various types of posts is to play around and actually use them. But wouldn't it be nice if the posts were presented in a stylish fashion? You'll learn how to make that happen in the next chapter, where you'll dive into the Tumblr themes.

chapter 4

Choosing a Tumblr Theme

in this chapter

- Exploring themes and their options
- Understanding the differences between free and premium themes
- Free and premium themes that stand out

CHOOSING A THEME for your Tumblr site isn't hard in itself; the problem is finding just the one you want. Luckily it is the wide variety of options and not a lack of available themes that makes this a difficult task. This chapter teaches you about theme options, how to change your theme, and how you can find more themes for your site. I also introduce you to some of my favorite themes, both free and paid.

What Is a Theme?

The *theme* is the framework that controls how your site looks. When you start your Tumblr site, a default theme is applied, but you can change it to any other from the Customization screen, as mentioned in earlier chapters. There are both free and premium, or paid, themes available directly from Tumblr, but you can also download themes from other sites and paste them into your site as code. You can also build your own themes, which you'll do in Chapter 10.

Behind every theme is a mixture of HTML, CSS, and Tumblr's own markup code. This code controls how your site is displayed in different situations, from the front page post listing, to showing a particular post. You'll learn more about the use of theme code in Chapters 9 and 10.

In short, the theme is the look and feel of your site, the skin if you will. Which theme you pick is entirely up to you.

 You need to be logged in to Tumblr to select a theme or alter your theme's settings. While logged in, from your Dashboard click the Customize link in the right column. This will take you to the customization screen for your selected Tumblr site.

Theme Options

Before we move on to the actual themes and how to find them, you need to learn a bit more about theme options. We touched on the most basic site options in Chapter 2, but theme options are different because they are unique to each theme. One theme might let you fill out your Twitter username for automatic inclusion, while another is ready for Disqus and lets you type custom CSS. The settings for each theme depend on the theme developer, so there are no general rules. You will, however, recognize a lot of these settings from theme to theme.

Take a look at the theme settings for the default theme, also known as Redux. Figure 4-1 shows the Tackling Tumblr blog, with the default theme.

FIGURE 4-1: Tackling Tumblr theme options

To review the theme options, open Tumblr and log in if needed to display your Dashboard. Click the Customize link from the menu on the right. You might think that the Theme tab would be the one to use when setting theme options, but that's not the case. As Figure 4-2 shows, the Theme tab is where you can browse themes directly from the customization view.

Click the Appearance tab to find the theme options, which can be many or few depending on the theme.

Theme options vary from theme to theme, but the way they are presented are pretty much universal. The Redux theme is the default theme for Tumblr, so it makes sense to use it as a benchmark. Take a look back at the Appearance settings for the Redux theme, shown in Figure 4-1.

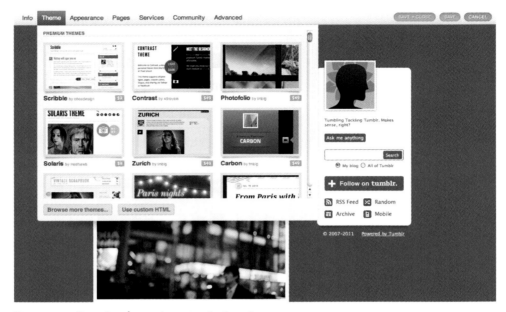

FIGURE 4-2: Browsing themes in customization view

You have the following options:

- **Background color.** Click the colored box to pick a completely different background color using a color picker or by writing the hex HTML code. Click the *X* to close the box and review other settings.

- **Title font.** You get a selection of web-safe fonts to pick from for the site title.

- **Body font.** Just like with the title font option, you get a selection of web-safe fonts. The body font is the text font used in the theme.

- **Accent font.** In this theme the accent font is used primarily for quotes and the like. Again, you get the same selection of web-safe fonts.

- **Header image.** Do you want to use a graphic instead of the site title in plain text? Then this is the button for you. Create the graphic on your computer and then upload it using the Upload button. This is a great way to further personalize your Tumblr site. (Note that your text title will no longer appear.)

- **Background image.** If you don't want a solid color as the site background you can upload an image instead. Either create one on your own or search the web for a suitable background image. There are tons of sites primarily offering background images for websites so you should definitely be able to find something that suits you.

- **Show People I Follow.** Tick this if you want to show who you're following. Not for the very private Tumblr user, obviously.

- **Show Tags.** If you're tagging your posts you should show the tags. Check this box to display your tags. Where the tags are displayed depends on the theme you have chosen, so consult the preview.

- **Show Album Art on Audio Posts.** This one's pretty cool; the theme tries to show off any album you publish with album art.

- **Enable Jump Pagination.** At the bottom of each page are the *Next page* and *Previous page* links. What if you want to show numbered pages instead? If you check this option, the user can both browse to the next or previous page, or jump to page 35 (or whatever) if he prefers. Figure 4-3 shows both alternatives.

FIGURE 4-3: Pagination with page jumps (top) and without (bottom)

Those are the options for the Redux theme, all pretty nice stuff that helps you personalize a commonly used theme. The background color and image settings in particular will help make your site unique, as will a custom header image. Just remember that the images you upload, whether a background image or a new header image, shouldn't be too large (in kilobytes) as not all your visitors will have your super speedy Internet connection.

Changing the Theme

Now that you've whet your appetite, how about actually changing the theme? Still in the customization view, now is the time to click the Theme tab. You'll get a dropdown window where you can browse themes, preview them right away by clicking them, and then either pick another or save the changes. Figure 4-4 shows Tackling Tumblr with a different theme applied, instead of the Redux one shown previously.

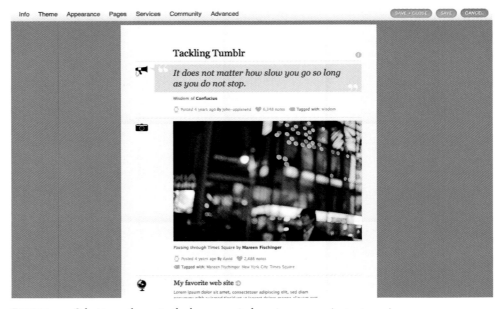

FIGURE 4-4: Selecting a theme in the browser window gives you an instant preview

At the top in this theme browser are the *premium* themes, which cost money. Below them you'll find the free ones, as shown in Figure 4-5. There's a great selection of both free and premium themes, so chances are you'll find several nice options fitting your site right here. But you're not limited to these themes; there are more in the Theme Garden.

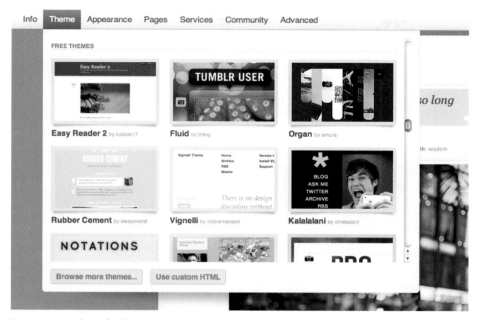

FIGURE 4-5: If you don't want to pay for your theme, just scroll down to the free section

The Theme Garden

The Theme Garden, pictured in Figure 4-6, is the Tumblr theme directory, with both free and premium themes for your perusal. Not all themes are available through the theme browser in the customization view; that just wouldn't be user-friendly since there are close to 700 themes to pick from as I'm writing this. You can reach the Theme Garden by clicking the *Browse more themes* button in the theme browse window, or by going directly to http://www.tumblr.com/themes/.

The Theme Garden is the official gateway for Tumblr themes. Every theme here has been approved by the Tumblr crew, which means that they work and adhere to the Tumblr standards. That includes having a great design, and a quick look around will show that the theme approval team is pretty tough on that point. Anyone can submit a theme to the Theme Garden, but that doesn't mean that it will be made available. The Theme Garden moderators decide what is good enough and what is not.

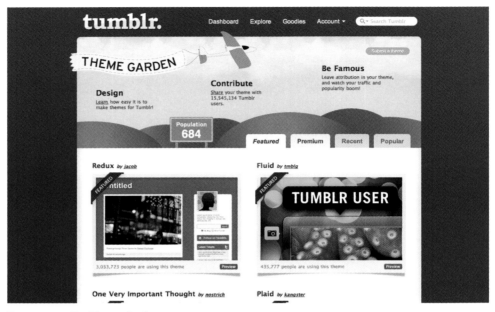

FIGURE 4-6: The Theme Garden

You can browse the Theme Garden in several ways, and also get some crucial data on the various themes. Premium themes cost money while others are free, so you get any pricing data. You'll also easily find out which themes are popular because there's a counter showing how many Tumblr sites are using each theme.

Figure 4-7 shows the Pink touch 2 theme (found at `http://www.tumblr.com/theme/16847`), which is free and can be installed with a click. Just make sure you're logged in, pick your Tumblr site of choice (if you have more than one), and then click *Install theme*. It's as simple as that!

There's also a *Preview* button so you can see the theme in action before actually installing it. Figure 4-8 shows a preview of the Pink touch 2 theme.

FIGURE 4-7: The Pink touch 2 theme in the Theme Garden

FIGURE 4-8: This is the Pink touch 2 theme

The *Preview* button opens a new window (or tab) in your web browser, so you can just close it when you're finished looking. Unfortunately you won't see the theme with your site, but with some dummy content. Tumblr will show you the theme with dummy content so you can preview how each post type will look. If you like what you see, just click *Install theme*; if not, continue browsing the extensive Theme Garden.

You'll find that a selection of the themes in the Theme Garden are available in the theme browse window in the customize view.

Custom HTML

There is a third option for Tumblr themes, sidestepping the Theme Garden altogether. Load up the customize view again, click the Theme tab, and then the *Use custom HTML* button at the bottom of the theme browse window. This replaces the theme thumbnails with a plain text code window showing a lot of code, as shown in Figure 4-9. What you see here is HTML code, and in Part IV of this book you will play a bit with the theme code.

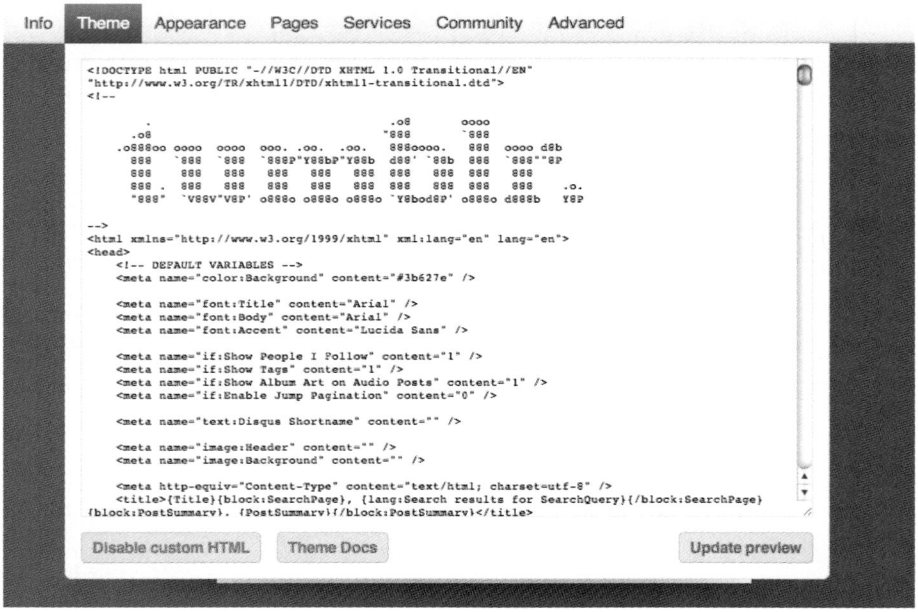

FIGURE 4-9: You can edit the HTML as well

Custom HTML is a great way for the HTML-savvy to edit the themes they like. You can also write your own HTML using the appropriate Tumblr tags, which we'll get to later as well. (If you can't wait, click the *Theme Docs* button, which will open Tumblr's own pages on the subject.)

There are some themes available online for downloading, meaning that you'd get a file with the necessary code that you can just copy and paste into the custom HTML window. Nowadays, most theme designers submit their themes to Tumblr for inclusion in the Theme Garden (although not all submissions are accepted for inclusion). However, some designers prefer not to, and instead make their themes available for download via their own site. Keep in mind that those "downloaded" themes might not meet Tumblr's standards. Another reason for not submitting to the Theme Garden would be to sell the theme on a different marketplace.

Free or Premium?

Should you pick a free theme, or pay for a premium one? That is a very good question, and one only you can answer. After all, it is your Tumblr site that needs a theme, and whether it is a free or paid one depends entirely on what you can find that suits you. Maybe there is a perfect free theme for you; then by all means use it. The same goes for premium themes; if you find the ideal theme you should consider buying it, assuming you can afford the expense. Luckily most themes aren't particularly expensive. You can find themes from as little as $9 US on the Theme Garden, and possibly even cheaper on other marketplaces. Premium themes in the Theme Garden are usually priced at $9, $19 or $49 US.

In short, pick a theme you like, and if it costs money, you'll just have to decide if you want to invest in the design for your Tumblr site or not. There is a third option: either design a theme yourself or hire someone to do it. The former takes quite some time, compared to picking a theme that is already available, whereas the latter can be quite expensive. Part IV covers Tumblr theming in more detail; if you want to design your own theme, Chapters 9 and 10 will help you get started.

Buying premium? Make sure you read up on the license terms. How many sites can you use the theme on, are there any other restrictions, will the theme developer offer support, and things like that — make sure you read and understand the terms before you pay.   **IMPORTANT**

A Nice Selection of Themes

With almost 700 themes to choose from in the Theme Garden, I figured you might want some help picking the cream of the crop. Design is in every way a matter of personal taste, so you might not agree with me on these themes, but at least the following two compilations of free and premium themes will give you something to stand on when you dive into the Theme Garden.

Without further ado, here are some nice themes for you to choose from!

> **NOTE**   Found a theme outside of Tumblr's Theme Garden? That means you will have to follow the instructions on the theme's site for how to obtain and use the theme. Usually that means downloading some code, and using the Custom HTML button in the customization view, as mentioned earlier in this chapter. See Chapter 9 for more information on how to edit a theme.
>
> When you find themes outside of the Theme Garden, make sure you preview them thoroughly so that they don't contain any weird code or links that you don't want on your site. Remember that themes acquired outside of the Theme Garden or a reputable theme company might not meet Tumblr's standards.

23 Sweet Free Themes

The themes in the following list are free to use on your Tumblr blog. They are all from the Theme Garden to ensure that they actually exist when you read this and that they are safe to use on your site.

- **Strict** (`http://www.tumblr.com/theme/107`) — Strict is a clean white and gray theme sporting a sensible color palette (Figure 4-10). It also has a cut title text, meaning that part of the title is hidden, which is pretty common on Tumblr themes. This theme works for both blogs and simpler sites thanks to the right column.

- **TumbleDesk** (`http://www.tumblr.com/theme/120`) — If you want your Tumblr blog to look like a desk where your posts are pages, this is the theme for you. The TumbleDesk theme is less suited for traditional sites. This type of design is relatively common in the blogosphere, and I think TumbleDesk is a decent choice if you like the visual style.

- **Chunky** (`http://www.tumblr.com/theme/5932`) — Chunky is a colorful theme with a strong header, which I like a lot. I'm not completely sold on the three column design because content with unbalanced length can make layouts like this look bad, but if you can find the balance then this is an impressive theme worth a closer look (Figure 4-11).

FIGURE 4-10: The Strict theme

FIGURE 4-11: The Chunky theme

- **Inkhorn** (`http://www.tumblr.com/theme/17428`) — Inkhorn has a clean look that I really like, but the content is split into two columns so you need to balance the length to make it look really good. Don't miss the excellent "back to top" stairway graphic in the lower right when you scroll down the page.

- **Royal Ribbon** (`http://www.tumblr.com/theme/11655`) — A nice color palette, pretty icons, and a lovely choice of title font makes Royal Ribbon a theme every Tumblr blogger should consider using. It is a bit tight at times, but overall it's really good choice.

- **Atonement** (`http://www.tumblr.com/theme/18246`) — Atonement is a modern take on the Tumblr blog, with great icons and nice use of whitespace between the content. It won't do for anything but blogs, though, so if you want a more traditional site running on Tumblr this isn't the theme for you.

- **Panda Classics Recycled** (`http://www.tumblr.com/theme/681`) — Concept themes are often hard to use, but I find I like Panda Classic Recycled enough to list it here. It takes its cue from the Penguin Classics books, making it a nice choice for book bloggers in particular. Obviously the color palette works perfectly on the screen as well.

- **Postage** (`http://www.tumblr.com/theme/6177`) — Postage has a strong graphic fixed at the top that you either like or not. The rest of the design is traditional Tumblr with a right column. This makes it easy to add links to pages and other stuff. Overall a nicely designed theme, worth a look.

- **Doodling in Class** (`http://www.tumblr.com/theme/8568`) — Another concept theme, this one pretending that your blog is doodled on a lined paper (Figure 4-12). Pretty nice actually, with "drawn" icons and everything. I find myself liking this one surprisingly much.

- **1000 Suns** (`http://www.tumblr.com/theme/531`) — 1000 Suns is a one-column theme with a nice color balance, with red and beige and white as the colors of choice. I do feel that unique icons for each post format would be preferable to the stars it uses (shouldn't it be suns?) but it is still a good option for the Tumblr-powered blog.

- **Rubber Cement** (`http://www.tumblr.com/theme/8758`) — Rubber Cement won't hit everyone's sweet spot, but personally I think it is one of the best free themes available on Tumblr to date. It works best as a traditional blog, but could actually work for a simpler site as well, thanks to the nice header and the top links (Figure 4-13).

FIGURE 4-12: The Doodling in Class theme

FIGURE 4-13: The Rubber Cement theme

- **Papercut** (`http://www.tumblr.com/theme/2807`) — A simple yet visual blog theme, Papercut delivers in both typography as well as the pretty icons. Worth a look for Tumblr bloggers, not so much for traditional sites.

- **Stationary** (`http://www.tumblr.com/theme/3292`) — Stationary is a clean theme that works both for traditional blogging and a simple site (Figure 4-14). The top part of the theme is really well balanced, making this one of the best options if you want a clean site on Tumblr.

FIGURE 4-14: The Stationary theme

- **Organ** (`http://www.tumblr.com/theme/9517`) — This is a really cool theme, with a completely different way of listing the content than you are used to. Organ is definitely not for everybody, but worth a look just because it is so cool (Figure 4-15).

- **Glacial Simplicity** (`http://www.tumblr.com/theme/14776`) — Glacial Simplicity is another excellent theme for the blogger on Tumblr. A nice header and balanced, toned down colors makes this an excellent choice for anyone tired of the clean white themes out there.

- **Effector Theme** (`http://www.tumblr.com/theme/17403`) — While I think the Effector Theme is a bit weak at the top of the site, it looks a lot better when you scroll down thanks to the header staying with the content. It's a clean and balanced theme with a right column, so this one's got a lot of possible uses (Figure 4-16).

FIGURE 4-15: The Organ theme

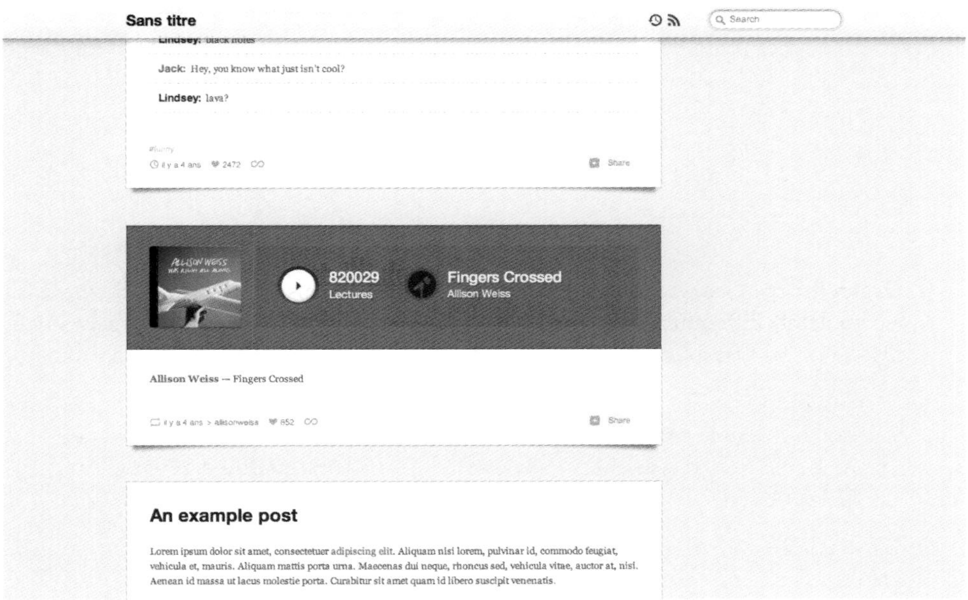

FIGURE 4-16: The Effector theme

- **Vertigo** (`http://www.tumblr.com/theme/370`) — Vertigo is a dark blog theme with very strong visuals. I especially like the cassette tape background for audio posts. It is one column, though, so you're pretty limited to blogging with the Vertigo theme.

- **Pink touch 2** (`http://www.tumblr.com/theme/16847`) — Another excellent option for Tumblr bloggers looking for a less obtrusive or overdesigned look. I do like the header on Pink touch 2, but I would prefer the site title in the top search bar as well, which is fixed when you're scrolling. A great theme overall, but hard to use for anything other than blogging.

- **Royal Cameleon** (`http://www.tumblr.com/theme/13331`) — Royal Cameleon (nope, that's not a typo) is a really visual blog theme that you either like or dislike. I'm not sold on it on longer text posts, but other than that it looks great to my eyes.

- **Esquire** (`http://www.tumblr.com/theme/368`) — Esquire is a theme inspired by the magazine with the same name (Figure 4-17). The visuals are strong and the left side is fixed when you scroll. I like it a lot, but am a bit reluctant to use it without some tweaking because it borrows so heavily from the magazine. The photo frame is lovely, by the way.

FIGURE 4-17: The Esquire theme

■ **Silo** (`http://www.tumblr.com/theme/11`) — Silo is a theme relying on boxes, with three per row, each containing a post (Figure 4-18). Since the boxes have a fixed height it doesn't look as broken when you mix different content lengths as two or three content column themes can do. It's a good option, although the typography could be improved.

FIGURE 4-18: The Silo theme

■ **for.screen** (`http://www.tumblr.com/theme/1355`) — If you want a dark blog theme, this one's for you. It shares the same layout as the default Redux theme (which you've seen repeatedly already in this book so it's not listed here), and could be used for simpler sites as well, although the visuals surely imply "blog" rather than "website."

■ **101** (`http://www.tumblr.com/theme/483`) — 101 is uncommon as a left-centered theme, standing out with its play on colors and the site title in the bottom right corner (Figure 4-19). Not for everybody, but I like it.

FIGURE 4-19: The 101 theme

17 Nice Premium Themes

All themes in the following list are found in the Theme Garden. You can buy Tumblr themes from other places as well (delivered as code that you use with the *Custom HTML* button), but because marketplaces come and go, swap owners, and so on, I've chosen to include only premium themes from the Theme Garden in this list. By all means, consider premium themes from places other than the Theme Garden, but be careful and research the reseller before paying anything.

> **NOTE**　When you buy a premium theme on the Theme Garden you get the license to use it on the Tumblr site you buy it for. You're not allowed to move the theme to another site, even if you own it. Themes are sold on a per-site basis, at least at this time, as premium themes are in beta for now. This might very well change, so be sure to check out the Terms of Service at http://www.tumblr.com/terms_of_service for the most up to date information.
>
> Prices noted for premium themes are in U.S. dollars.

- **Simplefolio** (`http://www.tumblr.com/theme/8955`, $49) — This is a nice portfolio theme that plainly shows how Tumblr can be used for managing your very own portfolio (Figure 4-20). Worth a look, I'd say, despite the fairly high price tag. You might also want to take a look at Photofolio (`http://www.tumblr.com/theme/8954`, $49), which is similar but geared toward photographers.

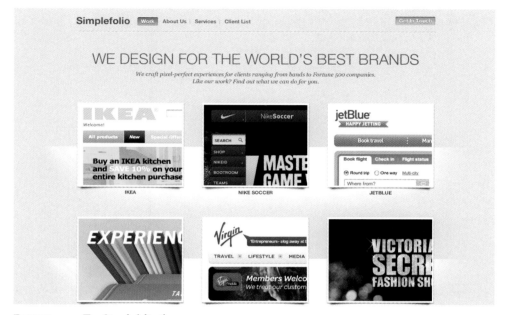

FIGURE 4-20: The Simplefolio theme

- **Solaris** (`http://www.tumblr.com/theme/8950`, $9) — Solaris is a well-designed theme for the Tumblr blog that just doesn't want to look like everybody else. We've seen almost everything from this one elsewhere, but nevertheless it is a nice design and a well put-together mix.
- **Rank & File** (`http://www.tumblr.com/theme/8952`, $49) — I love the way the Rank & File theme mimics a magazine; it is a clean design that should work for a lot of different projects (Figure 4-21). The price might be a bit steep, but I must say that this one looks worth it.

FIGURE 4-21: The Rank & File theme

- **My Corner** (`http://www.tumblr.com/theme/11721`, $19) — My Corner is a clean and good looking one-column theme focusing on your content. I like this a lot, with strong typography and spacing where it is needed (Figure 4-22).

- **Southern Afternoon** (`http://www.tumblr.com/theme/11418`, $49) — With lacy designs and a an old-fashioned Southern look to it, Southern Afternoon is definitely not for everyone. However, this is quality artwork in action right here, so if it fits your needs and you don't think you'll tire of the graphics, then by all means get it.

- **Sonic** (`http://www.tumblr.com/theme/8956`, $49) — The Sonic theme is geared for music bands (preferably ones with drumsets, with the graphic and all), and as such I think it does a pretty good job showcasing how Tumblr can be a great tool for a band (Figure 4-23).

FIGURE 4-22: The My Corner theme

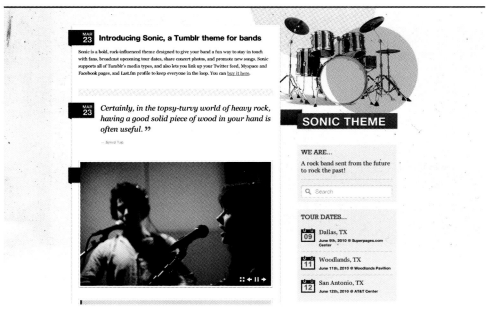

FIGURE 4-23: The Sonic theme

■ **Scaffold** (`http://www.tumblr.com/theme/8951`, $9) — While I find the Scaffold theme to be a bit messy at times, it is a pretty nice look if you have the right content for it, which would be something that can balance itself out over the two columns.

■ **Mars** (`http://www.tumblr.com/theme/26587`, $49) — Mars is a good looking modern take on a Tumblr blog (Figure 4-24). Chances are you'll like it, at least if you use a slightly less obtrusive background image than the one used in the showcase.

FIGURE 4-24: The Mars theme

■ **Carbon** (`http://www.tumblr.com/theme/16510`, $49) — Another good looking theme that stands out from the run of the mill. If you like dark designs you should definitely check this one out.

■ **Nova** (`http://www.tumblr.com/theme/13085`, $49) — This theme is pretty interesting with a distinctive design as well as several appearance settings. There's something called an "HD mode," which really means that the content is presented in just one wider column instead of the more typical two-column design. Still, pretty cool theme.

■ **Backburner** (`http://www.tumblr.com/theme/9391`, $19) — If you're looking for a more traditional blog look-and-feel, with a ton of icons and rounded corners for everything, then Backburner might be for you. Personally I find it a bit cluttered, but you could tweak it to fit your needs so it gets a mention.

- **Zurich** (`http://www.tumblr.com/theme/21756`, $49) — If you love yellow and the Helvetica font, then you definitely need to take a look at Zurich (Figure 4-25).

FIGURE 4-25: The Zurich theme

- **Carte Blance** (`http://www.tumblr.com/theme/14330`, $49) — Addicted to index cards? No, me neither, but that's the gimmick in this theme. Visually appealing, but as with every heavily designed theme relying on graphics like this one does, it might get old quick.

- **Fluid 2** (`http://www.tumblr.com/theme/15063`, $49) — Borrowing from Apple's icon design, using transparent glass effects and a bunch of rounded corners, you get a pretty cool theme with Fluid 2.

- **MagTheme** (`http://www.tumblr.com/theme/10625`, $19) — MagTheme wants to borrow from print media and create a better Tumblr experience. That means you'll be flipping pages, and it actually works pretty well. An interesting, different theme, worth a look if you're thinking of rolling your Tumblr site as something of a magazine (Figure 4-26).

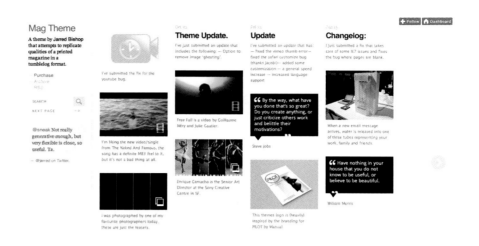

FIGURE 4-26: The MagTheme theme

- **Nautical** (`http://www.tumblr.com/theme/9376`, $49) — Another great looking theme relying on strong visuals, which might or might not get old fast for you. This one stands out, that's for sure.

Summary

Hopefully this chapter has helped you find the perfect theme for your Tumblr site, and if not at least you know where to look. Picking the right theme can be really hard, so later in the book (in Chapter 9) you'll learn how to edit a theme to truly fit your needs.

In the next chapter, we move on to the social aspects of Tumblr.

chapter 5

Networking with Tumblr

TUMBLR IS NOT just a publishing platform, it's something of a social network as well. This chapter discusses the social features within the platform and explains how you can follow and "like" other members' content and add to ongoing discussions. While Tumblr isn't Facebook or Twitter, you can still gain a lot by participating in the social parts of the service.

Among the social features of the Tumblr platform you'll find *likes* and *reblogs*, which we explore in depth in this chapter. You'll learn about the Ask feature, the option to have a direct question-answer relationship with your readers. You'll take a closer look at having multiple authors, or members, for a Tumblr site, and end with an overview of the various Tumblr trends that you're bound to come across.

The Tumblr Community

It is hard to pinpoint what we mean by *the Tumblr community*. Direct communication between users isn't key. Instead, you communicate by "liking" content other users publish to their Tumblr sites, you reblog that content on your own Tumblr sites, and you follow other people's updates through the Dashboard. Actual conversation between people only happens if a site has a comment feature enabled (that'd be Disqus, covered in Chapter 7) or allows visitors to ask questions using the Ask feature.

Despite those caveats, there's no doubt that there is a Tumblr community and that it is a social network. The traditional conversation isn't at the center, but rather a way of interacting through content.

Finding that content, and the people producing it, can be a bit tricky. A great way to get started is the Tumblr Directory, found at http://www.tumblr.com/directory/, which sorts Tumblr sites into various categories. A fun thing with the directory is that you'll be directed (no pun intended) to a random section when visiting it; you might be sent to the Comics section, as shown in Figure 5-1, or to Food, or News, or wherever. Click the triangle next to the current topic (Comics, in Figure 5-1) to see an index of all the directory topics.

Following Tumblr Sites

Your Dashboard is populated not only by your own posts, but also the posts from Tumblr sites you *follow*, as you can see in Figure 5-2.

FIGURE 5-1: The directory is a nice way to find new Tumblr sites to follow

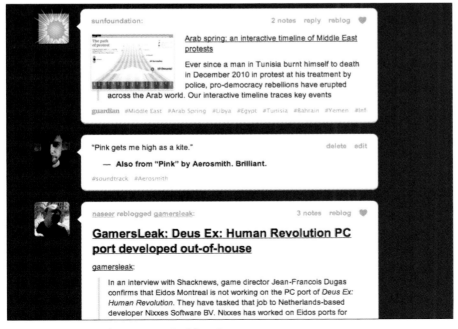

FIGURE 5-2: A mix of posts in my Dashboard

Following a site is easy. From the site, whether it's the front page or a single post you stumbled into, just click the *+Follow* button (see Figure 5-3) in the top right. You'll need to be logged in for this to work, otherwise Tumblr won't know who you are. If you're a Twitter user you'll recognize the behavior; it is very similar.

FIGURE 5-3: The Follow button

If you follow a large number of sites you'll have a lot of posts showing up on your Dashboard, and that can be daunting. To avoid an information overload that might make you overlook the content you really want to see, it's a good idea to follow only those Tumblr sites you're truly interested in and just visit others from time to time.

Your Dashboard is also the home for notifications of who is following you. New followers will show up in your Dashboard amidst the regular content. Obviously "following" notices are tailored to the Tumblr site you have selected (in the right column), so if you pick another blog, your Dashboard will look different. Tumblr blogs don't follow each other, users follow Tumblr blogs, so while you'll get blog-specific notifications of people following that particular blog, it is still the user that shows up as the follower.

You can stay up with the latest posts on Tumblr within the Tumblr network by subscribing to posts using RSS feeds or simply visiting them, but following is a great way to keep up to date with what's going on within Tumblr. It's also a way to tell a site publisher that you like the site, because when you follow someone he'll be notified. That will bring attention to you and your Tumblr site(s), so it may work to your advantage.

 TIP You can see who's following you by clicking the Followers link in the right column in the Dashboard. Remember that followers are tied to your Tumblr sites, so you'll have different followers for each site.

Liking Posts

There are two ways to help promote posts on Tumblr sites: liking and reblogging. To *like* a post, simply click the heart icon (see Figure 5-4) usually found in the top right of every Tumblr site. That's it: a click and you liked the post. You must to be logged in for this to work. The heart, initially white, changes to red after you like a post. The heart might not always appear; it is possible to hide it in the theme. It is also good to remember that you can't like a whole blog, just single posts, and you can't like posts on your own blogs.

FIGURE 5-4: The Like icon (heart) is in the top right

When you like a post, that information is usually displayed below the post. It all depends on the theme of the Tumblr site where the post resides, but this is the common practice. Likes are public information; everyone can see that you liked the post, so that's something to take into account. The red heart in the top right of Figure 5-5 shows that I liked that post; the same info might also be displayed in a list along with other users liking (or reblogging) the post, depending on the theme.

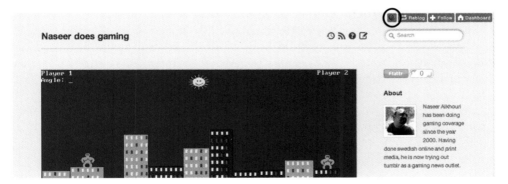

FIGURE 5-5: I liked this post, as the red heart indicates

Depending on which theme you use, the posts you've liked might show up in a list or other format on your own site. Keep that in mind, as you might not want to give some sites that kind of exposure.

NOTE

Reblogging Posts

Another way to promote other people's posts is by *reblogging* them. You can reblog by using the *Reblog* button in the top right on the post page, as shown in Figure 5-6. Clicking the *Reblog* button opens the write post screen, which will vary depending on the type of content you're reblogging. If it is a photo you'll do a photo post, and so on.

FIGURE 5-6: The Reblog button

NOTE The *Like* and *Reblog* buttons will be displayed only when viewing a single post, and won't be displayed on the homepage. From the homepage, you can only click the *Follow* button or go to your Dashboard.

When you reblog a post you'll get a quote tree filled out in the contents field. It shows who did what first, who reblogged it, who reblogged the reblog, and so on. Figure 5-7 shows a contents field with some reblogged content and my comment at the bottom.

FIGURE 5-7: Reblogging a post

How you reblog is up to you. Although you will get a tree filled out in your contents field, along with other data from the post such as click-throughs on images if there are any, you can edit it all. It's your post now, so you can do whatever you want with it. However, it is deemed bad form to not credit the source; some people even see it as stealing if you reblog without keeping the post's history in the content.

After you've reblogged a post you are returned to the actual post again, so you don't need to open additional windows or anything when clicking the reblog button.   **NOTE**

Ask Me Anything

The Ask page is a nice little feature that you activate from the theme customization screen, under the Community tab. When the option is enabled, an Ask link is added to your site, which you can name "Ask me anything" or whatever you like. Visitors can click the link to ask you questions using a simple form. You can set the options to require that users be logged in to ask a question, or allow questions from anonymous visitors, as shown in Figure 5-8.

FIGURE 5-8: Enabling the Ask feature

With Ask enabled, your users might ask you anything at all! That means that you might get valid questions, interesting insights, or complete and utter nonsense through the Ask form, especially if you allow anonymous questions. How the actual form looks depends on your theme, but it will probably be something along the lines of the one shown in Figure 5-9. You'll find it by adding /ask to your Tumblr site's URL, for example, http://tackling. tumblr.com/ask for Tackling Tumblr. Most sites that have Ask enabled will obviously link it as well, saving you the effort of typing it manually.

Submitted questions show up under Messages for your Tumblr site, found in the right column. From there you can answer them, either publishing the answer right away or choosing to queue the answer (see Figure 5-10).

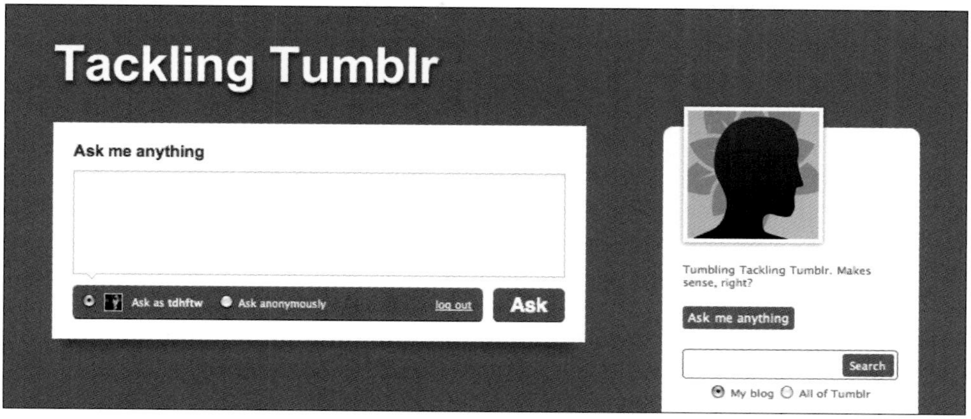

FIGURE 5-9: The /ask page for Tackling Tumblr

FIGURE 5-10: Answering a question

The question will show up in the content flow, along with the answer when published. The same question shown in the form in Figure 5-10 can be seen on the Tackling Tumblr site in Figure 5-11.

FIGURE 5-11: The question and answer on the site

> **NOTE** You do not have to enable the Ask feature. If you don't want to answer questions, or if your content is of the nature that won't generate questions, you may prefer to leave it off. Should you post something controversial, you might end up getting a lot of complaints or even abuse from the Ask form. You'd have the same problem with comments, of course.
>
> Before enabling the Ask feature, make sure you want to talk to your readers this way. There's nothing that says that you're a bad Tumblr user if you don't have the /ask page, so think about it before you enable. Luckily you can just disable the feature (without deleting the already published questions and answers) at any time.

Members

You don't have to update your site all by yourself; the Members feature allows invited users to add content to your site. Click the Members link in the right column in your Dashboard to go to the Members page, shown in Figure 5-12. Here you can add additional users who will be able to post to your site. Simply enter an email address to send an invitation to your prospective members.

> **NOTE** At this time you cannot invite people as members to your primary Tumblr site; you'll have to create additional sites if you want a group blog.

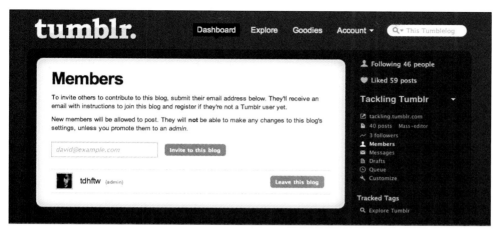

FIGURE 5-12: The Members page

Members who accept the invitation will see your Tumblr site among their own sites, and can now post to it. Pretty nifty. However, they can't change the site settings unless you make them administrators (*admin* for short), which would give them the same privileges on the site that you have. This is done from the Members page, where you'll see a *Promote to admin* button that lets you promote a user to admin.

This means that Tumblr sites work well both as group blogs and as traditional websites where several people need to be able to update the site. That's especially good for companies that don't have a dedicated web editor who handles all the publishing. Share the load!

Don't give anyone who doesn't really need it admin privileges. If a member of your site would like to hurt you they could do so more easily if they have admin privileges. Another problem would be if a fellow admin on your site has his account hacked or compromised, your site would also be at risk.   **NOTE**

Tumblr Trends

Tumblr is an interesting platform with some notable trends when it comes to the content. One oddity, for example, is the ridiculous number of bacon-related sites within the network. Trends obviously come and go, but these seem to stick around.

A nice way to get an overview of what the Tumblr editors think is hot is to visit the Explore page at `http://www.tumblr.com/explore` (shown in Figure 5-13), which picks out content for you and provides you with a list of popular tags. It is well worth a visit if you're looking for some new sites to follow.

FIGURE 5-13: The Explore page

F***yeahs

There are a lot of Tumblr sites with the word "f***yeah" in their names and URLs, usually combined with another term (the actual names use the full expletive rather than asterisks). An example is `http://f***yeahcats.tumblr.com`, publishing pictures of — you guessed it — cats. This type of phenomenon is called an Internet meme, a concept that spreads virally online (see `http://en.wikipedia.org/wiki/Internet_meme` to learn more about memes).

When browsing Tumblr you'll no doubt end up at one of these niched f***yeah sites. It's an interesting phenomenon, that's for sure, and sometimes garners amusing sites usually consisting of images and/or video content.

Want to find f***yeahs? There's a funny site called `http://isitafyeah.com` that will help you; just type a word or phrase to search.   NOTE

Bacon

For some reason there are a lot of bacon-oriented blogs on Tumblr. While bacon surely is delicious, it has become something of a joke online. If you want to keep up with the latest things bacon on Tumblr, by all means keep a close eye on the "bacon" tag which surely will lead you to the tastier sites publishing bacon content: `http://www.tumblr.com/tagged/bacon`.

Arts and Illustration

Tumblr appeals to a lot of people interested in art, illustration, and photography. This could very well be because most Tumblr sites are aesthetically pleasing in and of themselves, or perhaps it is the reblogging features that work especially well for images. Either way, there are a lot of Tumblr blogs specializing in artful photography, in illustration, and in other types of art.

There are a lot of possible tags to browse for art-related topics. One that recently caught my eye was the "Black and White" tag, full of black and white photography: `http://www.tumblr.com/tagged/black-and-white`.

Animated GIFs

Tumblr sites are often very visual and many include a lot of image and video content. Animated GIFs certainly aren't unique to Tumblr, but they do often find their way into Tumblr blogs. GIF is an image format that can be an animation, often appearing crude and pixilated because GIF files have a limit of 256 colors. The files also tend to be very slow to load if they are too detailed, so they are not the ideal format for showing off moving images. Most animated GIFs are spoofs of some kind, showing a captured sequence of something funny. Some are short movies or just silly animations.

For a selection of more or less amusing animated GIFs, check out the "GIF" tag: `http://www.tumblr.com/tagged/gif`.

NSFW

NSFW is short for Not Safe For Work, and is a moniker for content that might be considered inappropriate for viewing at work. Usually that means nudity or extreme situations that not all people are comfortable with. Whether you're comfortable with sharing the fact that you're looking at content like this is obviously up to you.

Pornography is the most common type of NSFW content, and it is a big niche on Tumblr, as it is on many platforms. Many Tumblr sites include pornographic photos, animated GIFs, or video clips.

Running an NSFW site yourself? You can mark your site as NSFW by setting it as NSFW under the Advanced settings in the customization view for your theme, as shown in Figure 5-14. Not all Tumblr sites with explicit content engage this setting, I'm afraid, so don't count on it when surfing the shadier parts of Tumblr.

IMPORTANT   Using the NSFW setting will *not* offer a warning to your visitors; it is only for the Tumblr directory, found at `http://www.tumblr.com/directory/` — at least for now.

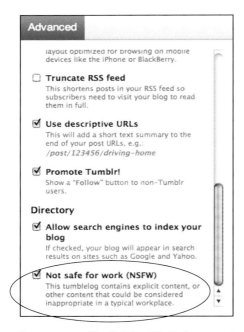

FIGURE 5-14: Not Safe For Work theme settings

Summary

You don't have to engage in all the community features of Tumblr to get a lot from the service itself and your Tumblr site(s). However, there are quite a few gains to be had from engaging with your fellow Tumblr users. For example, if you find someone whose content you enjoy, following this blog will not only add the updates to your Dashboard, it will also notify the blog owner of your interest. That in turn could lead to a refollow of one of your blogs. Reblogging is even more powerful since it will not only share content with your readership, but also show up in lists on the original post as a note that you reblogged that particular post.

What I'm saying is that engaging the Tumblr community can be a good idea, even a strategic one. And that's not counting the fact that you might enjoy yourself in the process!

In the next chapter you will focus on how you can connect your Tumblr sites to other social networks such as Twitter and Facebook.

Connecting to Other Services with Tumblr

TUMBLR ISN'T ALL about its own ecosystem, with following, liking, and reblogging. You can also import content from other platforms, whether it is a social network or another site you might be publishing. In fact, Tumblr makes it easy to do so.

This means that you can feed your content to social networks such as Facebook and Twitter, which can be a great way to keep your followers there up to speed automatically. You can also use RSS feeds from external sources and post them on your Tumblr site, which can be very handy if you have other blogs or sites that you want your Tumblr followers to notice.

Feeding to Facebook and Twitter

Given the overwhelming popularity of Facebook and Twitter these days, you will more than likely want to share your Tumblr content — from serious posts to a video of a cat chasing its tail — on your other social network accounts. Luckily, Tumblr makes it easy to communicate your content with both these fine social networks. Here's how you make it work.

Feed to Facebook

With Tumblr there is no need to rely on third-party services that publish content from an RSS feed to Facebook. Instead, click the Customize link in the right column from your Dashboard to get to the customization screen. From there, click the Services tab and then the *setup* link to the right of the Facebook heading, as shown in Figure 6-1.

> **NOTE**   RSS stands for Really Simple Syndication. Most modern websites publish an RSS feed as a way for people to subscribe and receive content. Instead of visiting your favorite sites every day to read their latest articles, you can subscribe to their RSS feeds (via Google Reader, using your web browser's built-in features, or using stand-alone software) and the content from those sites will be delivered to you. Your RSS reader acts as a centralized place to receive content and news. It really is a simple syndication solution for web content, making it easy for you to follow numerous sites on the same place.

Clicking the *setup* link sends you to Facebook, where you're prompted to log in should you not already be logged in (you obviously need a Facebook account for this to work). Here, Tumblr asks for your permission to publish to your Facebook account. Click the blue *Allow* button, shown in Figure 6-2. (If you're using Facebook in a different language you'll get a different screen.)

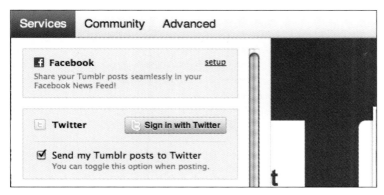

FIGURE 6-1: This is where you get started setting up your Facebook connection

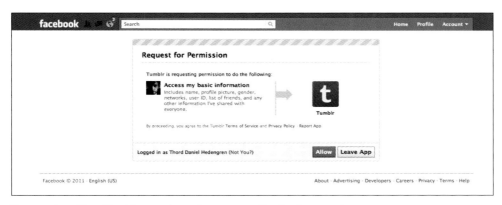

FIGURE 6-2: Allow Tumblr to make updates to your Facebook account
Facebook © 2011

Next, you're prompted to add the address to your Tumblr site, to be published to your news feed. In the case of Tackling Tumblr, it's `tackling.tumblr.com`, as shown in Figure 6-3. Enter your Tumblr site's address and click *Start importing this blog*.

Next you're prompted to allow Tumblr to post to your wall and do other things with your account; click *Allow*. If all goes well you get a message that posts to your site will be automatically imported into your news feed, which is to say your updates on Facebook.

That is all there is to it. When you publish a post to your Tumblr site, it will also show up in your Facebook news feed. Figure 6-4 shows an example.

FIGURE 6-3: Enter your Tumblr site's address
Facebook © 2011

FIGURE 6-4: A Tackling Tumblr update in my news feed on Facebook
Facebook © 2011

Don't want to import to Facebook anymore? You can disable the application by finding it in your app listing on Facebook and clicking the little X that shows up when you hover over the link. You'll get a prompt where you can alter the settings of the import (shown in Figure 6-5), or you can remove it using the *Remove and Block Tumblr* link in the bottom left of the dialog. Using that option, however, will hide all Tumblr updates from you, including those other people might do, so that's not the best route. Instead, go back to the setup page via the theme customization view (as you saw in Figure 6-1) and then click the *Disable and reconfigure* link. That's all there is to it.

FIGURE 6-5: You can remove and block the Tumblr Facebook app altogether if you like
Facebook © 2011

If you want to import to a Facebook page rather than a regular user, go to `http://www.tumblr.com/docs/en/facebook_pages/` (shown in Figure 6-6) and click the Connect with Facebook link. Select the page you want to import to, and then follow the instructions. It's just as easy as connecting Tumblr to your Facebook user, and you already know how to do that!

FIGURE 6-6: Connect your Facebook page

Feed to Twitter

Pushing content to Twitter is done in a similar fashion as with Facebook. From the customization screen, click the *Services* tab and then the *Sign in with Twitter* button found below Facebook (refer back to Figure 6-1). Twitter prompts you to log in, as shown in Figure 6-7; just as with Facebook you need an account to publish to.

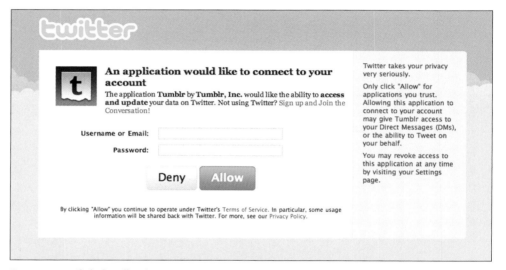

FIGURE 6-7: Click the Allow button
©2011 Twitter

When you log in with your Twitter account by clicking the Allow button, you are redirected back to the customization screen on Tumblr. Then you'll see that your Twitter account is linked with the Tumblr site you're editing, as shown in Figure 6-8.

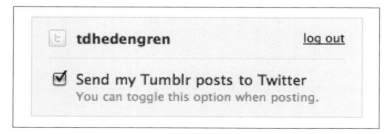

FIGURE 6-8: I have connected my @tdhedengren Twitter account with the Tackling Tumblr site

Now posts published to the Tumblr site will be tweeted as well. You can disable this connection at any time by clicking the *log out* link to the right of your Twitter handle (which is "tdhedengren" in Figure 6-8).

Connecting your Tumblr site to Twitter doesn't mean you have to publish everything automatically. In fact, you get to decide this on a post by post basis with the new checkbox called *Send to Twitter* that you'll find in the bottom right on all post writing screens, ticked by default and ready to go, as shown in Figure 6-9. Pretty handy, since you might not want to clutter your Twitter account with every little reblog you do.

FIGURE 6-9: You don't have to send everything to Twitter

Publishing RSS Feeds with FeedBurner

RSS feeds are a great way to subscribe to updates. Using RSS reading software or websites, users can get your content delivered as you publish it. If you want more details on how your RSS feed performs, how many are subscribing to it, and what kind of click-through rates it gives you, you can choose to use the FeedBurner service owned by Google. This not only gives you more details on how your RSS feed is being used, but also offers nice features such as e-mail subscriptions automatically created from your RSS feed. All in all, it's a pretty powerful tool.

NOTE   All Tumblr sites come with RSS feeds, so you don't need FeedBurner to let people subscribe
        to your site. However, by default there are no statistics on those RSS feeds.

A word of caution before we move on to enabling the FeedBurner feature for your RSS feed. When people subscribe to a feed, they subscribe to that feed's address. Using FeedBurner means that they will subscribe to a FeedBurner.com address, and hence you will lose your subscribers if you choose not to use FeedBurner anymore. Obviously you can tell your readers to update their feed URLs in whatever software they are using, but you can't be sure that all will do that. You also need to know that FeedBurner isn't instantaneous, meaning that it will take some extra time (30 minutes or so) before your content shows up in the FeedBurner feed, compared to the time it would take for it to be available in your default RSS feed.

TIP   Did you know that you can truncate your RSS feed? If you don't want your readers to get the
        full content when they subscribe to your RSS feed, check the *Truncate RSS feed* option in the
        Advanced tab on the customization screen. Be careful though; people prefer to get the full
        feed rather than a cut version.

To use FeedBurner you need a Google account. If you already have a Google account you can just log in to FeedBurner at `http://feedburner.com` using your Google account info. Otherwise now is a great time to set up a Google account; you can register for one at `http://feedburner.com.` Once you have the account, you can log in to FeedBurner.

After logging in, paste the address to your RSS feed in the input field under the "Burn a feed right this instant" heading on the front page. *Burning a feed* simply means telling FeedBurner that you would like them to handle the RSS feed traffic and publishing. Once supplied with the address, FeedBurner will create a new feed for you to give to your readers. This is the URL you will want to give your readers so they can subscribe and receive your latest content. Your Tumblr site's URL to the RSS feed is the actual Tumblr site URL with an added `/rss` after it. So for Tackling Tumblr, found at `http://tackling.tumblr.com`, that would be `http://tackling.tumblr.com/rss` — easy enough, right? I've added that to the input field on the FeedBurner website, as shown in Figure 6-10.

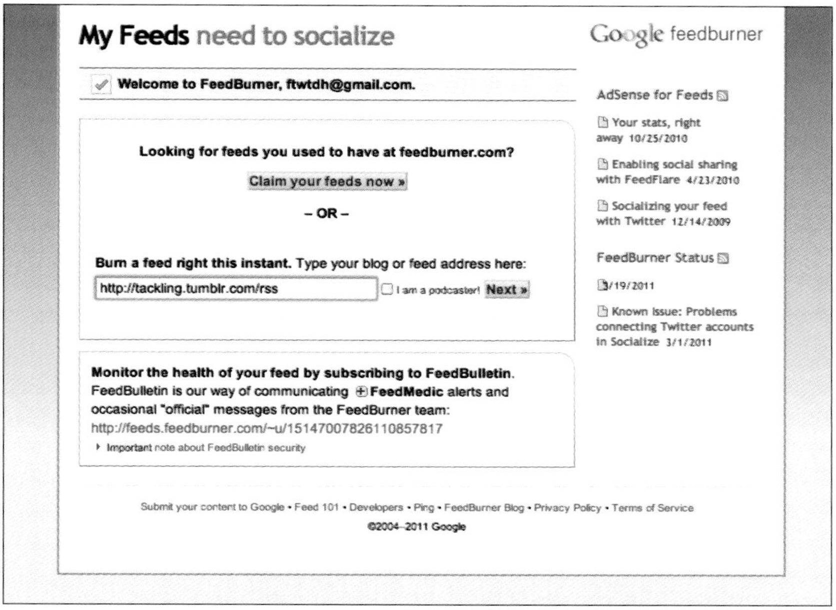

FIGURE 6-10: Getting ready to burn my feed
©2011 Google

You can ignore the *I am a podcaster* option (unless you are, in which case you need to read up on what gives with that, as it depends on how you want to publish your work), and just click the Next button. This brings you to a simple settings page where you can set the Feed Title and the Feed Address. I'm happy with my defaults, shown in Figure 6-11, so I just click the Next button again.

That's it; you have successfully burned your feed on FeedBurner! There are a ton of settings and cool tools here, so by all means explore the site. Two features that merit attention are the statistics for your feed and the e-mail subscriptions option. If you enable the statistics features, you'll get data about your site such as how many of your feed subscribers clicked on links. The e-mail subscriptions option allows your readers to subscribe via e-mail to a news-letter containing a digest of your feed's content. Not all people are happy with RSS readers, so that is a nice alternative.

FIGURE 6-11: Basic feed settings
©2011 Google

To start using the feed, you need to go back to the Services tab of the customization screen and paste the FeedBurner URL in the FeedBurner field, as shown in Figure 6-12. Save your settings, and that really is all there is to it.

FIGURE 6-12: My FeedBurner URL added

Other Services that Work with Tumblr

Not everything is about feeding *from* Tumblr. Maybe you have content that you want published *to* a Tumblr site as well. Perhaps you have a blog somewhere that you want to automatically show up in your Tumblr stream of content when you update it, or maybe it's something entirely different you want to expose. Either way, as long as there is an RSS feed that you can use, Tumblr can publish it for you, and luckily most services provide an RSS feed these days.

Adding such content is easy. Open the customization screen and click the Services tab. Scroll to the bottom to find *Automatically import my . . .* (see Figure 6-13), under which you will find a few items to play with.

By default there are two dropdown items; the left says *RSS feed*, and the right says *Links*, as shown in Figure 6-13. Below these two is the *Feed URL* field, as well as a button to start importing it. If you change the left dropdown to YouTube, the right one disappears and the bottom field will ask for your YouTube username instead (see Figure 6-14).

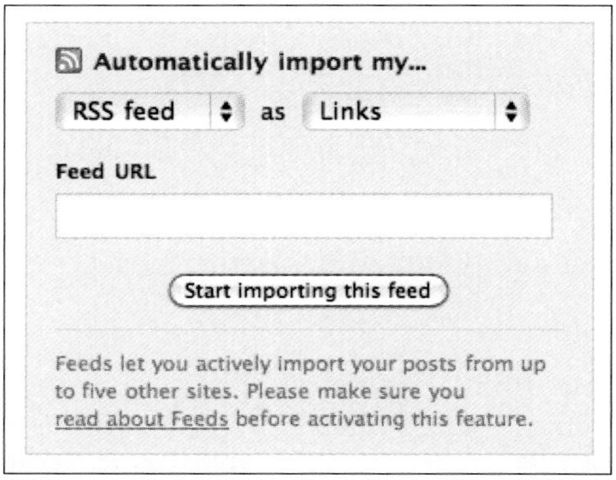

FIGURE 6-13: You can import to Tumblr as well

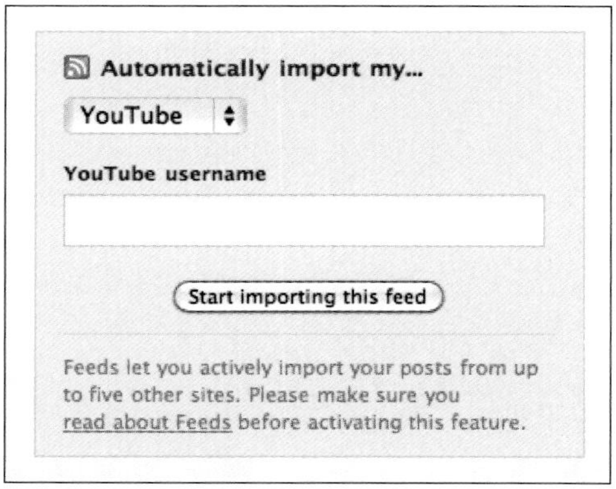

FIGURE 6-14: YouTube just wants your username, nothing more

The left dropdown enables you to choose the kind of content you want to import. The right dropdown is for how it should be published on your Tumblr site, meaning the post format you want to use. If your type of content only includes one post format type, the left drop-down list will disappear, as with the YouTube example, since Tumblr is intelligent enough to understand that YouTube consists only of videos.

These are the services you can import from, and the information you must provide for each service:

- **RSS feed** — feed URL needed, you set the post format
- **Del.icio.us** — username needed, published as links

- ■ **Digg** — username needed, published as links
- ■ **Twitter** — username needed, published as texts
- ■ **WordPress.com** — blog name needed, you set the post format
- ■ **Blogger** — blog name needed, you set the post format
- ■ **LiveJournal** — username needed, you set the post format
- ■ **Vimeo** — URL needed, published as videos
- ■ **YouTube** — username needed, published as videos

Adding services is easy. Just fill out the necessary information and click the *Start importing this feed* button. It says *feed* for everything, by the way, because that's what Tumblr actually pulls from these various sources.

You'll find all your imported sources below the button in a nice little list. Here you can also click the red X next to each source to remove it from your Tumblr should you want to. You'll also see when the next import is due (see Figure 6-15).

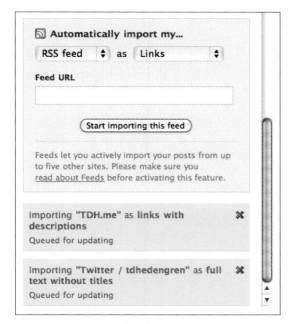

FIGURE 6-15: This is what I'm importing to my Tumblr right now

Can I Move My Site to Tumblr?

Of course you can! Just point your domain to Tumblr (using the settings under Info on the theme customization screen) and then get started posting! Unfortunately, Tumblr does not support any kind of true import from other platforms at this time. You can republish content from Twitter, Facebook, and so on, but moving a complete site from another publishing platform just isn't possible yet.

If you do decide to move to Tumblr you either have to start fresh, or do it the hard way, by copying/pasting the entire site. If you choose the latter, make sure that your old links are redirected to their new home. How you go about doing that depends on what platform you're moving from. Chances are that a little scripting could solve it if you're self-hosted, but if you rely on a hosted platform you're pretty much out of luck.

Summary

It is probably tempting to push all your content to Twitter and Facebook, and likewise import any content from external sites to your Tumblr blog using RSS, but you should consider all the implications. Will your Twitter followers enjoy getting tweets about your Tumblr posts, for example? And do your Tumblr followers care about the content you import using RSS? Ask yourself these questions before utilizing all these excellent tools.

Chapter 7 moves on to another type of communication, the comment functionality.

chapter 7

Working with Comments on Tumblr

THESE DAYS JUST about every page on the Web urges you to interact and leave a comment with your thoughts, opinions, and feedback. This practice sparks some great conversations and brings new ideas to the table, but it can also be a nuisance and a bore. In this chapter I discuss Tumblr and comments, and show you how to enable them for your site. You will learn about the Ask feature and how it differs from traditional comment functionality. You'll also learn how to enable Disqus comments on a site using a theme that supports it.

Comments versus Asks

You learned about the Ask feature in Tumblr in Chapter 5. Asks are general question boxes that your readers can use to send you a question about whatever is on their minds, just as they would via any contact form on a website. Instead of sending an e-mail to the site owner and getting a private reply, asks publish both question and reply on the site.

Comments and asks aren't the same thing. *Comments* are tied to a particular post (or page), so the idea behind enabled comments is to open up an avenue for discussion and feedback on a *per post basis*.

It might come as a surprise, but Tumblr doesn't have a native comment system. When you start your Tumblr blog you can't just click "allow comments" to let people speak their minds and rip your content to pieces. Instead you have to rely on third-party solutions if you want comments in the traditional sense.

Keep in mind that a lot of reblogging is really commenting on that same content, much as you'll see in Figure 7-1. When reblogging, the content is usually quoted (that's good form, as we've covered already), and then the reblogger adds a thought or two on the subject. That same thought might just as well be submitted as a comment, but with a reblog you get the benefit of wider distribution because it is posted on the reblogger's Tumblr site as well. However, with the absence of a private channel to discuss the topic you lack actual communication with the reblogger.

In a way, the Tumblr ecosystem has already solved the lack of traditional comments with reblogs and likes, and those who need comment functionality can get it with the integration of Disqus (covered later in this chapter). If that's not enough, Tumblr also has a Reply feature for your followers, which we'll also get to later. All in all, traditional comments still add value to a Tumblr site, as with any other site, but you must decide whether you need to enable a comment feature.

FIGURE 7-1: This reblog includes the original content, plus a comment

Should You Allow Comments?

Why would you want to have comments on your Tumblr site? You might think that between likes and reblogs, perhaps topped off with the Ask feature, you'd have all you need when it comes to user integration. Comments, though, open up new possibilities, in part because they are limited to the post they are attached to.

Whether or not you choose to support comments is entirely up to you. It is important to think this decision through. You can change your mind later, but enabling comments and then suddenly removing that feature may look bad and leave readers wondering why it was removed, so think about the issue carefully.

Advantages of Comments

Here are some reasons to allow comments on your posts:

- **Encourage discussion.** Getting the input of your readers might lead to new areas of interest, increased knowledge, or just an enjoyable discussion on a topic.

- **Open floor.** Letting other voices speak on your site shows that you're open to input and interested in what others might think. Most people see that as something positive, and that can increase interest in your site.

- **Support.** Let's say you release Tumblr themes and post about them. If you have comments enabled, your visitors could ask you support questions there, and sometimes other readers will answer them before you will. Plus, the answers are shared with others who might have the same questions. It's a much more efficient method than answering a ton of e-mail asking the same question, that's for sure. (Asks can also work well for support.)

Disadvantages of Comments

Comments are not always positive. Here are some reasons not to allow them on your posts:

- **Spam.** This is a serious issue in the blogosphere today, and while most commenting systems have spam protection, some unwanted bits do come through. If you enable comments you have to be prepared to handle spam.

- **Harassment.** Both span and harassment are annoying, but spam is generally automatic and aimed at a large, non-specific audience, while harassment is intentional harm directed at someone specific. You or some of your readers might be harassed by other readers. You must address these situations if you want to avoid losing readers.

- **No comments.** This is a tough one. Not every post will have a comment. In fact, a lot of blogs in the blogosphere have next to no reader interaction at all, despite comment fields. People comment when they are angry or extremely happy, and while having no comments really doesn't have to mean anything, it is disheartening and can look bad.

Comments are a good thing in the right place, especially if you want to encourage visitors to react to your content. Whether your site would benefit from allowing comments is something you'll have to decide for yourself.

Hosted Comment Solutions

Tumblr doesn't offer a built-in native commenting solution that you can just enable, like those on other platforms such as WordPress or Blogger. Instead you'll have to rely on third-party services that take care of the comments for you. This can have its advantages because a lot of things that might be complicated to activate, such as commenting using your Facebook profile, will work right away. There are disadvantages as well, such as not having your own copy of the comments.

There are several hosted comment solutions available. The leading ones are:

- Disqus (`http://disqus.com`)
- coComment (`http://cocomment.com`)
- Echo (`http://aboutecho.com`)
- IntenseDebate (`http://intensedebate.com`)
- Facebook comments (`http://developers.facebook.com/docs/reference/plugins/comments/`)

These hosted commenting solutions all work in a similar fashion, so which one you choose depends entirely on which interface you prefer, and possibly what features you want to prioritize. This book covers only Disqus, for two reasons. First, Disqus is by far the most common hosted comment solution, which means that both you and your readers might be familiar with it. Second, built-in support for Disqus is available in quite a few Tumblr themes, which makes it an easy and natural choice.

What does it really mean to have hosted comments? It means that your comments reside on the provider's server. Much like your posts live with Tumblr, your comments will exist on the provider's servers and be loaded from there. While that won't be a problem most of the time, keep in mind that if your comment provider goes bankrupt you will lose your comments. Most, if not all, hosted comment providers will let you export the comments, so if the worst happens you can revert to the exported comments.

> **IMPORTANT**
>
> Using a hosted comment solution means that your site's comments are stored someplace other than your actual site. This means that if your hosted comment service of choice should go out of business, not only will your comments stop working but they will also be lost. Luckily, there are export features available that let you download a file containing all your site's comments. That means that you can move them to another service or keep a local copy. The hosted comment solutions listed here have all been around for some time, one way or another, and I deem them safe to use. However, it is good to know that should the worst happen you can at least save the comments and try to move them someplace else.

Using Disqus for Your Tumblr Comments

While Disqus (`http://disqus.com`) is not the only hosted comment solution, it is by far the easiest one to add to your Tumblr site (see Figure 7-2). A lot of Tumblr themes make it really easy to add Disqus comments just by supplying the Disqus shortname, as you'll see in a little bit. The themes that don't offer this functionality will need some minor additions in the code.

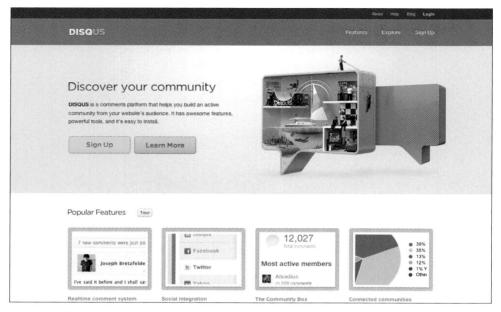

FIGURE 7-2: The Disqus homepage
Copyright 2007-2011 DISQUS

Getting Started with Disqus

First you need to register an account with Disqus. Each account can have several sites attached to it, so get an account for yourself and then add the site(s) you want. Signing up is a breeze; you just provide the required information, as shown in Figure 7-3. You'll find the sign up link on the Disqus website (`http://disqus.com`), or you can go directly to `http://disqus.com/admin/register/`.

If you already have a Disqus profile (because you have other sites using the service or maybe you just commented on a Disqus powered site and registered a profile then), this screen will look slightly different (see Figure 7-4). You can reach it from `http://disqus.com`, or via the Add site link to the right in the Disqus Dashboard.

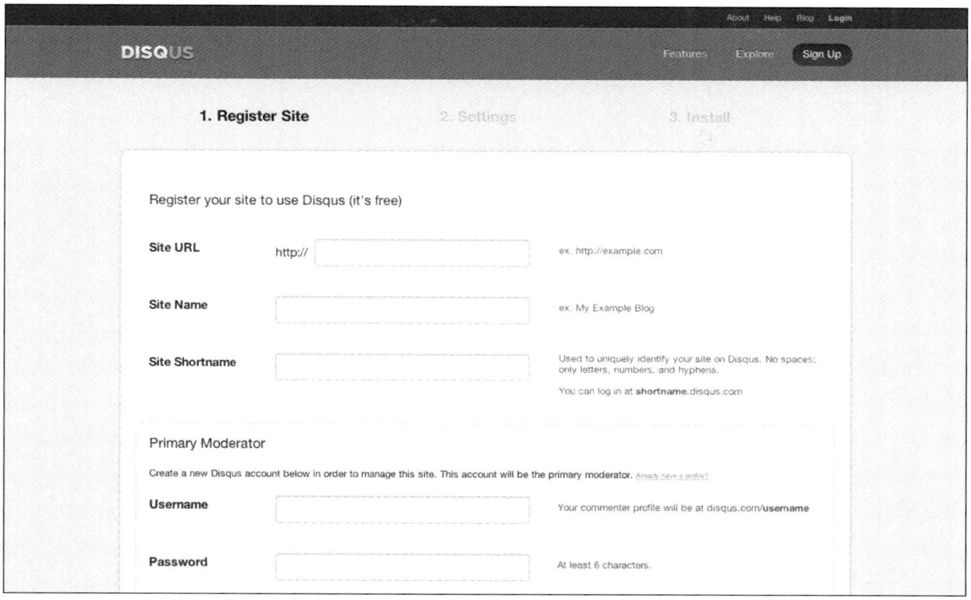

FIGURE 7-3: Signing up for Disqus
Copyright 2007-2011 DISQUS

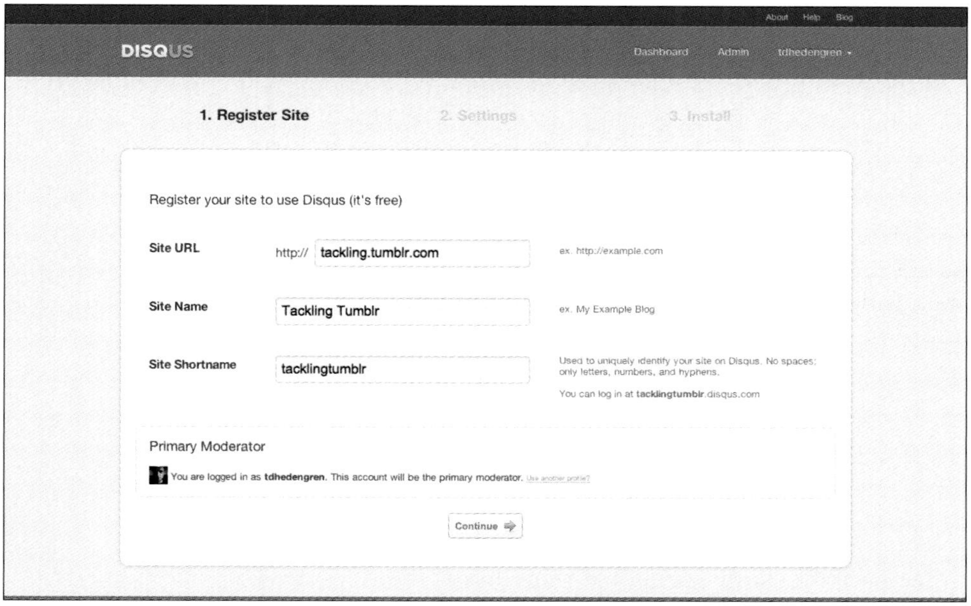

FIGURE 7-4: Signing up with a user account
Copyright 2007-2011 DISQUS

I filled out the details for Tackling Tumblr in Figure 7-4. Click *Continue* to proceed with a quick setup of the site. Figure 7-5 shows the Quick Setup screen, step 2 in the Disqus signup procedure. In a lot of cases these are all the settings you need.

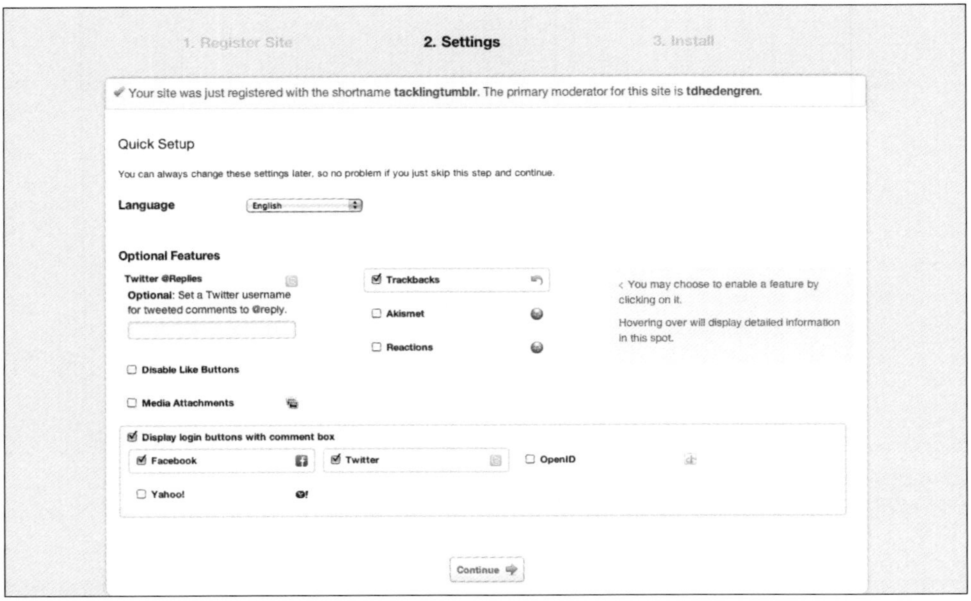

FIGURE 7-5: Setting up the Tackling Tumblr Disqus
Copyright 2007-2011 DISQUS

Notice in Figure 7-5 that I want to allow commenting using both Facebook and Twitter profiles. This is all handled by Disqus, so you won't have to worry about setting up Twitter or Facebook apps to make this work.

Click *Continue* again to display the Install screen (Figure 7-6). Here you'll find install details for a lot of different platforms. Clicking the Tumblr link will send you to a page with instructions for using Disqus with Tumblr. You can do that, of course, but you don't have to — keep reading!

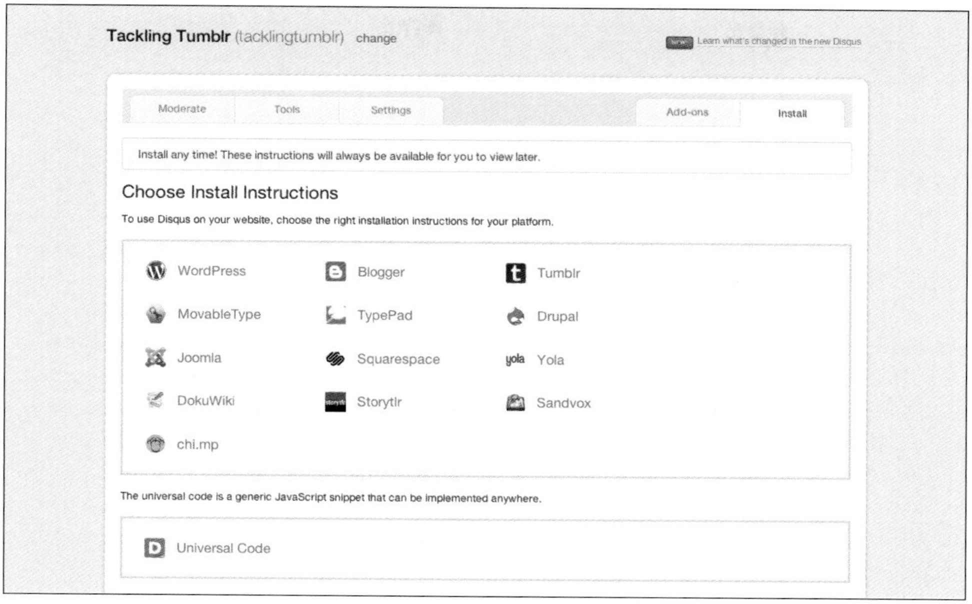

FIGURE 7-6: Time to install the Disqus code
Copyright 2007-2011 DISQUS

That's all there is to signing up for Disqus. You can check out the Disqus Dashboard (see Figure 7-7), found via the Dashboard link in the top menu, for an overview of the activity on your various sites. Clicking a site name under Your Sites in the left column leads to the appropriate settings panel (which you can also reach via the Admin link). From there, click the change link to the right of the All sites title in the top left. The Settings tab on the Admin page offers the same site selection procedure should you have several sites attached to your Disqus account. Figure 7-8 shows the site selection process via the Admin page.

You can make other Disqus users moderators of your comments if you like. Under Admin → Settings, click *Moderation* in the left column and then *Add a moderator*. Share the load with your trusty friends.

TIP

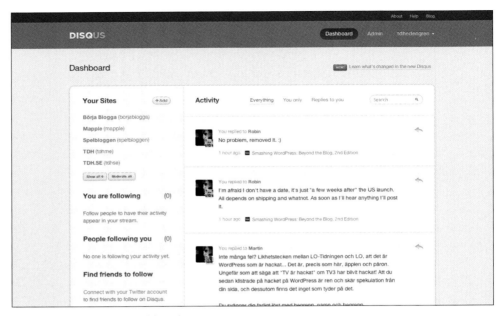

FIGURE 7-7: The Disqus Dashboard
Copyright 2007-2011 DISQUS

FIGURE 7-8: Picking the site from the Admin screen
Copyright 2007-2011 DISQUS

Enabling Disqus on a Tumblr Site

A lot of themes, including the friendly Redux one you've seen so many times already in this book, support Disqus out of the box. That means that all you need to do is supply your Disqus shortname (the one for your registered Disqus site, not your username), and save to get Disqus comments on your site. For Tackling Tumblr, that was "tacklingtumblr" as shown in Figure 7-4.

Go to the customization screen via the Customize link in your Tumblr Dashboard and click the Appearance link in the top menu. As shown in Figure 7-9, you have a box for your Disqus shortname, which again is the site shortname, not your username. Fill it out and then click Save.

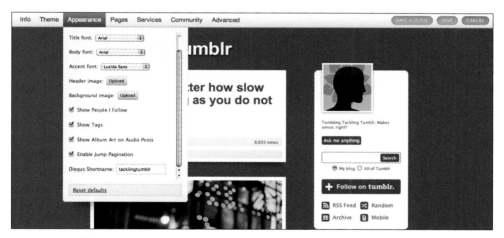

FIGURE 7-9: Fill out your Disqus site shortname

That's it; you now have Disqus comments enabled on your site. Figure 7-10 shows how it looks on a single post page for Tackling Tumblr.

FIGURE 7-10: Disqus enabled on Tackling Tumblr

Disqus in the Theme Code

What about themes that lack the Disqus site shortname box in Appearance? Can't you get Disqus comments on those? Of course you can; it just involves some fiddling with the theme code, which might be a little too much for some users.

In Tumblr, you will need to add two Disqus code blocks to your theme code, via the Custom HTML option under Theme on the customization screen (see Figure 7-11). Every theme is different, which means that there is no universal solution to exactly where in the theme code you add the Disqus code blocks. I cover theme code more thoroughly in Chapters 9 and 10, but if you're familiar with HTML you might be able to track down the right place to paste the code snippets.

Go back to Disqus, log in, and click Admin in the top right. From there, click the Install tab and scroll down to the manual instructions (Figure 7-12).

FIGURE 7-11: You need to insert code into your theme using the Custom HTML view

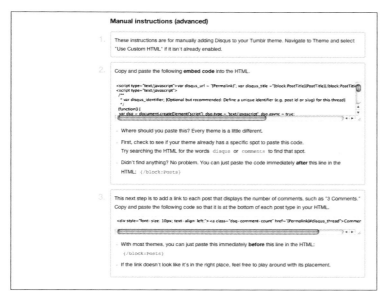

FIGURE 7-12: The manual (advanced) installation instructions

The page shows two blocks of code. The first block, in step 2 of the instructions, is for displaying the Disqus comments. Copy this code and paste it where you want the comments to show up, usually below your post. The second code block, in step 3 of the instruction, is the comments link that tells the visitor how many comments there are for the post. Obviously you want that in a suitable place as well.

Is this the ideal way to add comments to a Tumblr site? No, it would be a lot better if all Tumblr themes were Disqus-ready, but unless you're prepared to switch to a theme that is, you'll have to add the Disqus code to your Tumblr site manually.

Enabling Replies

The Reply feature, added as a beta feature in April 2011, is not the same thing as comments. Replies are allowed only for people you follow, and as I'm writing this, the only way you can use replies is from the Dashboard. There, when enabled, you'll find a reply link next to the number of notes and the reblog link (see Figure 7-13).

FIGURE 7-13: Replies in the Dashboard

Clicking the link opens up a reply area where you can comment on the post in question, as shown in Figure 7-14.

To enable this feature for your site, just click the Customize link in the right column from your Dashboard to get to the customization screen. Open the Community menu at the top of the page, and check the boxes for allowing replies as shown in Figure 7-15. Save your changes and you're all set.

FIGURE 7-14: Write a reply

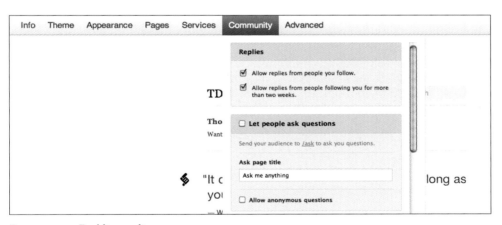

FIGURE 7-15: Enabling replies

By the time you read this, chances are that you can do more things with the Reply feature, as it was in early beta when this book was written, and worked only for the primary site for your account. Hopefully this is a much more compelling feature when this book is published.

NOTE

Summary

Whether you want to open the lines of direct communication with your readership through Ask and comments is up to you. While blogs generally offer commenting functionality, Tumblr does have other ways of interacting with the content, as you'll remember from Chapter 5, so you'll have to decide whether you will benefit from enabling comments.

Now that you know all about communicating with your readership, the next chapter takes you a few steps from traditional blogging to look at how you can create different kinds of sites using Tumblr.

chapter

8

Beyond Blogging with Tumblr

in this chapter

- Working with pages
- Using Tumblr for things other than blogging
- Learning how to post to your site outside of the web interface

THE TUMBLR PLATFORM can be used for more than just your average blog. In this chapter, you'll take a closer look at using Tumblr to power sites for small businesses, marketing, sites for the family, and more. You'll also learn how to use pages for your static content, and discover some widgets that can add features and functionality to your site. Finally, the chapter explains how you can post to Tumblr using apps, e-mail, and more.

Great Uses for Tumblr Sites

There are quite a few possible uses for a Tumblr site, way beyond the blogging that dominates the platform. In this section you take a look at some of these possibilities.

Using Tumblr for Small Businesses

I've touched on the possibilities with Tumblr in previous chapters, but this section will give you a more in-depth look at what you should consider when you're using Tumblr for a small business site. Obviously the same advice could very well apply for other kinds of sites as well, so keep an open mind.

First you need to decide what you want from your website. If you don't ever intend to update it, then Tumblr isn't the platform for you; you should just build something static and forget about it. Obviously that's pretty bad for search engine optimization, and people will most likely only find your site because you've advertised it in some fashion. Still, not all businesses need more than a simple page online with the necessary information (e-mail, phone number, open hours, perhaps a map) so while you'll no doubt get more visitors if you update your site, you shouldn't waste the time if there are no gains to doing so.

However, most small businesses have some sort of news flow that requires at least periodic updates:

- A store or retailer could post photos of new arrivals.
- A law firm could post about wins in court.
- A PR firm could post about its clients.
- A consultant could post about work done.

The list goes on and on. It all boils down to the needs of the business so these are just broad strokes.

Some things, though, are universal and should be present on just about any small business website. The following should most likely be pages, rarely changed but always present and easy to get to through a navigation menu:

- **About page.** Visitors should be able to read about the business, and perhaps get some history as well if you have something to tell.

- **Contact page.** It should always be easy for visitors (potential customers) to get in touch with your business. A contact page might also include physical addresses and a map.

- **Staff page.** People have more trust in companies that disclose who works there, so be sure to show off your talented staff, preferably with at-work contact information for everyone involved.

Those are the essentials. Other than that you might want to have pages, which we cover later in this chapter, about the kind of work you do (what you sell, what you develop, advice, and so on), who you've worked with, and the like. You'll use the posts and their content flow to post about work delivered to clients, talk about your new contract, announce that you've hired that talented person (and link to the staff page, of course), and so forth.

Why should a small business use Tumblr to do all these things?

- It's easy to set up.

- It's easy to update.

- It's easy to use a custom domain.

- There are tons of nice looking themes you could use as a basis.

- If you got the content, you can get traction from likes and reblogs from the Tumblr community.

A lot of stale and boring business websites could be vastly improved by using Tumblr instead of that legacy system that someone paid a ton of money for back in 2001. It's worth a thought for sure.

When starting a Tumblr site for a small business, consider what kind of regular content you could publish on the site. It might also be a good idea to put one employee in charge of updating the site, although the more that are involved, the better. | TIP |

Using Tumblr for Marketing

Tumblr is great for launching marketing sites focusing on one product (or a small brand for that matter). A straight marketing site has different requirements than a small business site, mainly because the site is most likely tied to a limited campaign. When the campaign is done so is the site; most likely it will just sit there unattended, which might not be the best thing but such is the reality of marketing.

Here's a list of reasons you should use Tumblr for your marketing endeavor:

- It's easy to set up and maintain.
- It's easy to modify, whether you're building on an existing theme or from scratch.
- It's possible that you'll get viral traction for the content you publish through the Tumblr users.
- It's easy to import content from other sources you might use in your campaign.
- You can connect any domain to Tumblr.

The true power in using a Tumblr site for marketing is the possible viral impact. If you post great content, others might reblog it, crediting your site.

> **TIP** Did you know you can embed your Tumblr site on a non-Tumblr site just by pasting a simple JavaScript? The JavaScript can be found on the Goodies page (`http://www.tumblr.com/goodies`) but always has this format:
> ```
> <script type="text/javascript" src="http://YOURSITE.tumblr.com/js"></script>
> ```

More Cool Uses for Tumblr

The possibilities for Tumblr are almost limitless. With some imagination you can build a lot of different sites using Tumblr, especially if you spice up the theme you've chosen with some additions of your own. We'll get to the custom theme stuff in the following chapters; for now all you need is your imagination and the will to create something.

Here are some possibilities to get your mind rolling:

- **Family site.** The ease of use of Tumblr, combined with the Members feature, makes the platform excellent for a family site. This way everyone can stay up to date on what's going on.
- **Personal site.** If you're trying to establish a reputation online and build your personal brand, a Tumblr site detailing your skills and services, along with a blog, is a good idea.
- **Artist portfolio.** We have already established that Tumblr is good looking. If you're an artist, whether your medium is photography or building sculptures using recyclable materials, you'll find Tumblr to be a great platform to present your work and yourself.

- **News site.** Whether you want to write about the latest gadgets or what's going on in your hometown, Tumblr offers a simple and fast interface to do so. There are nice themes for you to use as well.

- **Local team.** Are you coaching a little league theme or just playing football with your buddies on the weekends? A Tumblr blog for all things team related is a great way to keep both your fellow players and your fans up to date.

- **Group notebook.** Any project relying on teamwork can benefit from an online notebook, so why not use Tumblr for sharing all those links, photos, and quotes? Again, the Members feature is a great tool for this.

Another feature that might be handy is Ask, since that allows family members to ask questions and someone can answer, making sure that everybody has access to the information. Perfect for that "what computer should I buy?" question that pops up all the time.

Teach everyone to tag appropriately so that you can keep events and family reunions tied together. As you know, tags are keywords that describe the content, and they also offer an archive functionality. The tag "Hedengren Family Reunion 2011" would tie all the tagged posts together in an archive.

TIP

Some of these sites will benefit from additional features, such as pages and widgets. *Pages* are static pages outside of the post flow; *widgets* are code snippets that grab data from other services, such as your latest tweets or what music you're listening to. Let's start by taking a closer look at pages.

Making Better Use of Tumblr

Tumblr isn't just about publishing post after post. You can also add static pages to the mix. If that's not enough, you can spice things up even more by including code snippets from other sites and services you want to show off, such as Facebook fan page boxes and your latest tweets from Twitter.

Working with Pages

Most non-blog sites, and quite a few blogs as well, need informational pages, where visitors can go to learn more about the site, company, people, publisher, or whatever. Typical pages include an about page, a contacts page, a staff page, and so on.

As of March 2010, Tumblr supports adding pages. Pages live outside the post flow, so you won't create them using any of the post format icons on your Dashboard. Instead, click

Customize on the right side of the Dashboard. You'll find a Pages menu at the top on the customization screen (see Figure 8-1), which gives access to the Add a page link.

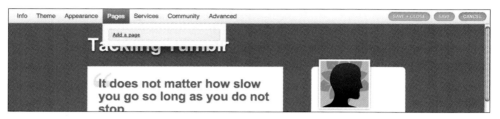

FIGURE 8-1: Add a page

Clicking the Add a page link opens a popup with familiar fields. Actually creating the page is much like writing a text post, but without the right column for tags, when to publish the post, and so on. Figure 8-2 shows the Add page popup window.

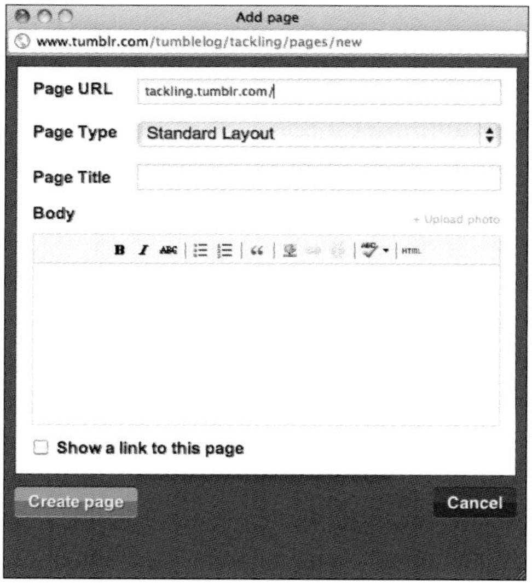

FIGURE 8-2: The Add page popup window

Upon close inspection you'll find that some fields on this dialog are different from regular text posts.

First you need to pick a Page URL, which is where the page is to be located. Your Tumblr site URL will be filled out here already, so you'll just add something that goes after that, much like you add a slug to your posts. Pick something that describes the page content, like "contact" for a contact page or "about" for an about page.

Next is Page Type, which is a dropdown select box where you can pick from three different page types:

- **Standard Layout** is a regular page, much like a text post. This is the default page type, as Figure 8-2 shows.

- **Custom Layout** removes the page title field and switches the editor to a box for Custom HTML. This can be very useful for advanced Tumblr users who would like the freedom of manipulating the page's HTML rather than sticking to the default page layout.

- **Redirect** lets you point the page URL entered in the top field to a different URL. In Figure 8-3 I've inserted a link to the Tackling Tumblr book page on TDH.me. This can be handy when you're working with several sites that belong together.

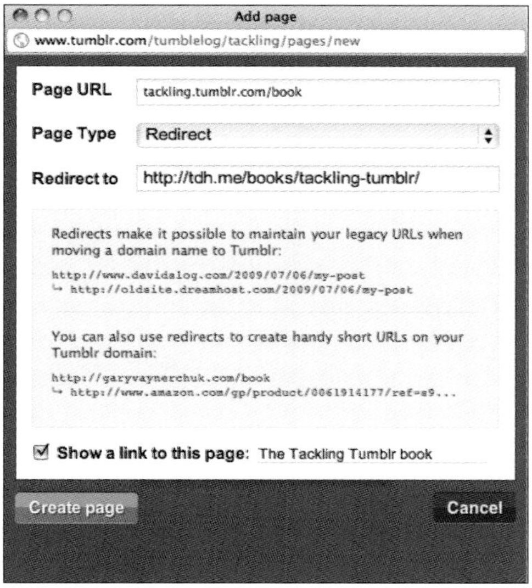

FIGURE 8-3: A redirect to the Tackling Tumblr page on TDH.me

All page types have the option to show a link to this particular page or not. If you don't check the box at the bottom left, the page won't be linked on your Tumblr site by default; you'll have to link it manually if you want your visitors to be able to find it easily. Depending on the theme you're using this might actually be preferable, but most themes have dedicated areas that will list your pages, so checking the Show a link to this page checkbox is usually a good idea.

Figure 8-4 shows the completed Add a page popup, for reference.

FIGURE 8-4: A simple presentation page for the Tackling Tumblr book, before clicking the *Create page* button

When you're done, no matter what kind of page you're creating, click the *Create page* button.

> **NOTE** Unfortunately you can't create a page as a front page for your site; you need to supply a new and non-existing page URL for the page.

Adding Helpful Widgets

If you're familiar with blogging platforms such as WordPress, you know all about widgets.

The term *widget* is used very loosely and it differs from platform to platform. Widgets are small little functions that you can add to your site; for example, your latest updates from Twitter, a slideshow of photos from Flickr, a Facebook fan page box, and so on.

The procedure for adding widgets varies according to your platform. In WordPress, for example, you add them by drag-and-dropping them to widget areas. Other platforms have areas where you paste code, but the end result is the same: A widget appears on your site. Tumblr doesn't officially use the term "widget" at all, because it has no widget system like WordPress. For our purposes, widget really can mean a Twitter widget (Figure 8-5), a Facebook fan page box, a box displaying the latest played tracks from Last.fm, and so on. *Widget* is really just a term used to pull all of these together under one roof.

FIGURE 8-5: Getting the Twitter widget from twitter.com (http://twitter.com/about/resources/widgets/widget_profile)
© 2011 Twitter

So in short, for the sake of this book, widgets are code snippets that you can copy from various sites and online services that offer them (such as Facebook or Twitter), and then implement on your site. I list a few nice sites that offer widget codes for your Tumblr site later in the chapter. But first, I'll show you how widgets work by adding my Facebook fan page box to the Tackling Tumblr site.

Adding a Facebook Fan Page Widget

In this example, I will add a box for my own Facebook fan page to the Tackling Tumblr site. My fan page can be found at http://facebook.com/tdhftw. You can follow along and add a suitable Facebook fan page box to your own Tumblr site, the process is more or less the same.

You can use the general procedure outlined here to add widgets to your own sites. The list presented at the end of this section provides URLs where you can find widgets for many social networking sites and other services.

NOTE

First I need the Facebook fan page widget code. Facebook offers code snippets for a lot of different things, so it needn't be a page to actually work. The element I'll use here is called the Like box, which lets you "like" my fan page directly from the box on the Tackling Tumblr site.

To get the code for my fan page, I'll go to `http://developers.facebook.com/docs/reference/plugins/like-box/`, where the dialog shown in Figure 8-6 displays.

FIGURE 8-6: Grabbing the Facebook fan page code
Facebook © 2011

The Platform page is filled out in the Facebook Page URL field by default. I want the Like box on my fan page instead, so I change the URL to **http://facebook.com/tdhftw/**. This changes the preview image to one for my page, as shown in Figure 8-7. I leave the other settings alone for now.

FIGURE 8-7: Hey look, my fan page
Facebook © 2011

Clicking the *Get Code* button opens a modal window (Figure 8-8) where you can copy either an iframe or a JavaScript code snippet. The latter, using XFBML, is usually preferable although either usually works for most publishers. If you pick the XFBML, you could get more usage data from your box, but it is entirely up to you. For the visitor, the result will be the same. Copy whichever of the snippets you prefer to use.

Your Like Box plugin code:

iframe

```
<iframe src="http://www.facebook.com/plugins/likebox.php?
href=http%3A%2F%2Fwww.facebook.com%2Ftdhftw&amp;width=292&amp;co
lorscheme=light&amp;show_faces=true&amp;stream=true&amp;header=tru
e&amp;height=427" scrolling="no" frameborder="0" style="border:none;
overflow:hidden; width:292px; height:427px;" allowTransparency="true">
</iframe>
```

XFBML

```
<script src="http://connect.facebook.net/en_US/all.js#xfbml=1"></script>
<fb:like-box href="http://www.facebook.com/tdhftw" width="292"
show_faces="true" stream="true" header="true"></fb:like-box>
```

Okay

FIGURE 8-8: Get the code
Facebook © 2011

Next, I have to figure out where I want the code, and then paste it there. I click the Customize link in my Tumblr Dashboard, leading to the customization screen. In the case of Tackling Tumblr, I'm still running the Redux theme so I have two options. I decide to try adding the fan page box to the right column, so I click Info in the top menu.

The Description field is what will be displayed in the right column in the Redux theme, and it takes HTML code, so I paste the Facebook fan page code there, as shown in Figure 8-9. Notice that I put some text at the top and wrapped it inside <p> tags (stands for *paragraph*, standard HTML), which is to make sure that text stays on a separate line. Clicking *Save* in the top right shows how the page looks with the widget in the Description.

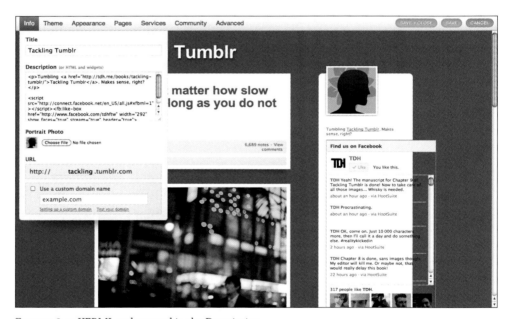

FIGURE 8-9: XFBML code pasted in the Description

As Figure 8-9 shows, that doesn't look too good. The Facebook widget is too wide to fit into the right column. A quick look at the HTML code of the theme (using the appropriate method to view source for your web browser of choice) tells me that there are 210 pixels to work with when it comes to the right column content width. So I can go back to Facebook and change the fan page box by adjusting the Width field from the default 292 to 210 (see Figure 8-10).

Now it's just a matter of clicking *Get Code*, copying the code, and going back to the customization screen to replace the code in the Description field. The end result is a Facebook fan page box that actually fits, as Figure 8-11 shows.

FIGURE 8-10: Now with the right width
Facebook © 2011

FIGURE 8-11: The Facebook fan page widget in place, and with the right width (http://tackling. tumblr.com/)

TIP Most Tumblr themes support adding HTML code, and hence widgets like the Facebook fan page box, to the Description, and then output them in an appropriate place. Obviously this is more common in themes that have two or more columns; one-column themes don't always use the Description box in a fashion that looks good with widgets like this. The best way to know is to give it a go and try for yourself with the theme you've chosen.

If you don't want to use the Description box and its designated place in the theme you'll have to edit the theme code and add the widget that way. I'll do that in Chapter 9, so stay tuned.

Widgets for Your Site

There are tons of services and sites that offer widgets of different kinds that you might want to add to your website. Following are several that might interest you:

- **Twitter** (`http://twitter.com/about/resources/widgets/`) offers several different widgets, from boxes with your latest tweets, to search results.

- **Facebook** (`http://developers.facebook.com/docs/plugins/`) has boxes for pages, profiles, comments, and more.

- **Flickr** (`http://www.flickr.com/badge.gne`) offers HTML and Flash badges showing off your photos in different ways.

- **ShareThis** (`http://sharethis.com/publishers/get-sharing-button`) gives your site sharing buttons for numerous social networks.

- **Last.fm** (`http://www.lastfm.se/tools/charts`) has widgets showing what you've been listening to.

- **Skype** (`http://www.skype.com/intl/en-us/tell-a-friend/get-a-skype-button/`) has nifty buttons that urge your readers to Skype you, if you'd like that.

- **Meebo** (`http://www.meebome.com/`) is a hosted IM client and you can embed it for instant messaging with friends and readers.

- **Google Talk** (`http://www.google.com/talk/service/badge/New`) can be added as a widget as well, for even more IM.

- **Tumbltape** (`http://www.tumbltape.com/`) is a pretty cool service that lets you listen to music (or other audio) from any Tumblr site, and embed it as a widget as well.

- **LinkedIn** (`http://developer.linkedin.com/docs/DOC-1072`) has a widget if you want to show off your profile from the business-oriented network.

- **LinkWithin** (`http://www.linkwithin.com/`) inserts thumbnails that link within your site, a pretty popular widget among bloggers in particular.

- **Amazon Wish List** (`https://widgets.amazon.com/Amazon-Wishlist-Widget/`) is a great way to show off your Amazon wish list — and with any luck, someone will buy you something from it!

- **Google Friend Connect** (`http://www.google.com/friendconnect/`) embeds a box that lets your readers connect using Google Friend Connect.

Don't overdo it. Too many widgets will make your site look cluttered, and that's neither pretty nor appealing to the user. Go for the ones you need, and leave the rest out.   `NOTE`

Additional Ways to Publish Content to Tumblr

You've spent quite some time in the Dashboard, posting content and whatnot. While the most surefire way to post to Tumblr sites is still through the Dashboard, that's not the only way to post to Tumblr. In fact, there are numerous programs that can post to the service, not to mention apps and bookmarklets. You won't find any links to unofficial software or apps here, though. Not because they are always lacking, quite the contrary actually, but because they aren't guaranteed to work with Tumblr all the time. If Tumblr changes something, their own official apps will be updated right away, but third-party apps might lag.

The Tumblr Apps

Native apps are the preferred method for a lot of people these days, and while Tumblr works well on most smartphones (and tablets) as is, the apps can offer a more optimized experience. There are apps for iPhone and iPod touch (but not iPad), Android mobile phones (requires Android OS 2.1 or higher at the moment), and Blackberry. You can find download links for these, along with other information, on the Goodies page at `http://www.tumblr.com/goodies`. Figure 8-12 shows Tumblr on the iPhone and Android platforms.

If you dislike the apps you can always post to Tumblr via e-mail; most mobile phones can do that these days.   `TIP`

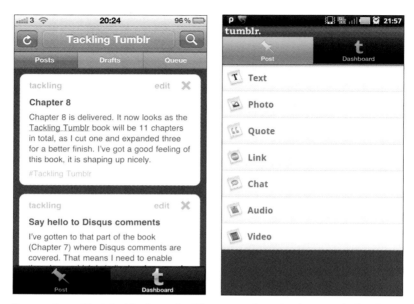

FIGURE 8-12: The left side shows the iPhone app, the right shows its Android equivalent

Using the Tumblr Bookmarklet

The Tumblr bookmarklet is an excellent way to post to your Tumblr site directly from pages when you're surfing the Web. You get it from the Goodies page, where you can drag the *Share on Tumblr* button to your web browser's bookmarks bar (you might have to enable that from the menus).After that, any time you stumble on something brilliant online that you want to post to your Tumblr site you can just click the Share on Tumblr link in your bookmarks bar, and it will open a popup (see Figure 8-13) where you can create the actual post! Plain awesome. Don't miss the Advanced link in the bottom right so that you can set tags, when to publish, and so on.

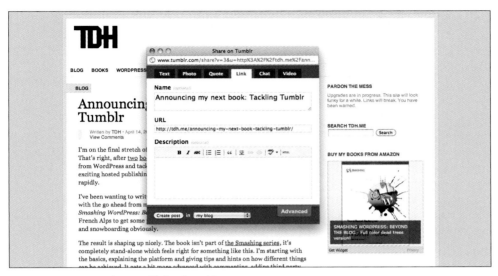

FIGURE 8-13: Using the Tumblr bookmarklet

Tumbling Using E-mail

You can use e-mail to publish to your Tumblr blog as well. Each blog has its own dedicated Tumblr e-mail address, which you definitely should not share with anyone since that's a gateway to your site! You find the e-mail address you should send your Tumblr posts to on the Goodies page. The one you see there is the e-mail address for your default blog; if you have several you need to click the *View the mobile addresses for your other blogs* link to get the others.

Sending in posts via e-mail is simple. Just compose the e-mail as you always do, where the subject is the title of the post and the e-mail message is the actual content.

- **Text posts** are plain e-mails with text in the message; the subject (which is to say, the title) is optional.

- **Photo posts** should have an image in the message. If you've got several photos, just put them all in the message.

- **Link posts** should have the URL in the message. Don't forget the subject; it's hard to click the link without a title.

- **Quote posts** should have the quote within double quotation marks, and any credit on the line below with a single line in front of it (see Figure 8-14), no subject.

- **Chat posts** are written just like regular chat posts, with each person on their own line.

- **Audio posts** should have an audio file attached.

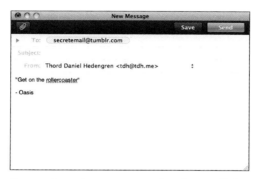

FIGURE 8-14: A quote post ready to be e-mailed

Pretty simple. You can't schedule or queue posts like this, but you can tag them by putting the tags somewhere within the message content, with a # in front of each. So #apples and #cake would add the tags "apples" and "cake" to the post.

| TIP | Don't forget to remove your e-mail signature from the message body if you append one automatically. That can look pretty silly on a site! |

Calling in Audio Posts

If you like you can actually call in audio posts. You'll find a phone number that you can call (a U.S. number) on the Goodies page. But before you can do that, you need to configure your phone number so that Tumblr knows who you are. To do so, just click the *Configure* button under the phone number to call, and fill out your phone number and possibly a PIN if you want the extra security (see Figure 8-15).

Calling in is easy enough, but a word of warning: If you're not in the United States this could get expensive quickly, so make sure you keep that in mind. International users should also make sure that international code for their country is in the configuration, as that is needed.

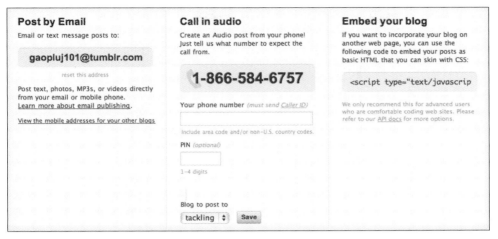

Post by Email

Email or text message posts to:

gaopluj101@tumblr.com

reset this address

Post text, photos, MP3s, or videos directly from your email or mobile phone. Learn more about email publishing.

View the mobile addresses for your other blogs

Call in audio

Create an Audio post from your phone! Just tell us what number to expect the call from.

1-866-584-6757

Your phone number *(must send Caller ID)*

Include area code and/or non-U.S. country codes.

PIN *(optional)*

1–4 digits

Blog to post to

tackling ♦   Save

Embed your blog

If you want to incorporate your blog on another web page, you can use the following code to embed your posts as basic HTML that you can skin with CSS:

<script type="text/javascrip

We only recommend this for advanced users who are comfortable coding web sites. Please refer to our API docs for more options.

FIGURE 8-15: Configuring the dial-in option

If your phone doesn't show a caller ID, Tumblr won't know who is calling, and hence can't publish your audio file. Make sure the phone sends a caller ID. If you're uncertain, consult the mobile phone's instruction manual on how to enable or disable this.

NOTE

Summary

Blogging is by far the most common usage of Tumblr, but as you can see there are plenty of alternatives. You can build just about any type of site that has a straightforward content flow, and thanks to the pages feature you can even keep your company presentations and other static content to itself.

It's time to dive into the theme code and learn how to customize your sites the way you want them.

part IV
Tumblr Theming

chapter 9
Editing Tumblr Themes

in this chapter

- Selecting the right theme
- Understanding Tumblr tags
- The typical Tumblr theme structure
- Editing Tumblr themes

CHANCES ARE THAT you won't find a Tumblr theme that looks and feels exactly the way you want it to, although you might get close. That's why this chapter tackles how to edit Tumblr themes. You'll learn how to pick the right theme for your needs, and all about the Tumblr tags that output the content from your Tumblr site. After that you'll get an understanding of how Tumblr themes are structured so that you can find your way, and finally you'll practice editing Tumblr themes.

> **NOTE**   This chapter is fairly code intensive (although not as intensive as Chapter 10, where you'll build a new Tumblr theme). You will need a working knowledge of basic HTML and CSS to follow the material in this chapter. If you are not familiar with HTML and CSS, or just need a refresher, Appendix A suggests some excellent books and online resources, and reviews some best practices. You don't need to be an expert in these markup languages to find your way around the theme code, but the more you know of HTML and CSS, the easier it will be for you to navigate the code.

Caution, Things Will Break!

As you edit your Tumblr theme, things will break, meaning that your theme suddenly might not look the way you're used to. If you remove an element from the theme code and save your changes, that piece will be removed from your site as well. That's why it is important to preview your changes when fiddling with the code, and to save your changes locally. This section shows how to avoid unnecessary headaches when working with themes.

The Working Environment

First, all theme editing takes place in the customize view, which you already know how to access. If you have several Tumblr sites you need to know which one is selected because that's the one you'll be customizing.

> **TIP**   The ideal way to test your edits is to have a test site with some appropriate dummy content. That way you don't risk making a live site look weird or broken should you mess something up. Remember, you can always create new Tumblr sites for your account, as you learned in Chapter 2.

To edit a theme's code, select the theme and then click the *Use custom HTML* button (see Figure 9-1). That brings up the code for the theme (see Figure 9-2), which you then can edit. If you need to leave the code view, click the *Disable custom HTML* button to go back to the theme list. If you click *Disable custom HTML* your edits will disappear.

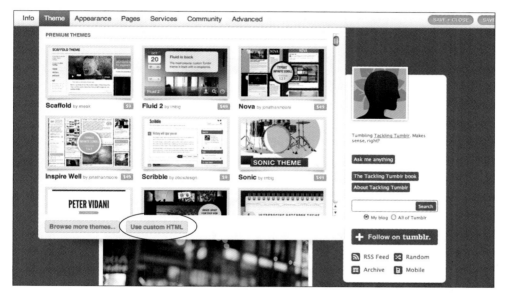

FIGURE 9-1: Click the Use custom HTML button to begin editing your selected theme

The *Update preview* button at the bottom right of the theme editing window is a great tool. Clicking it updates the site preview beneath the window, which is the only way to see how your alterations look without actually clicking any of the *Save* buttons at the top right. There's a huge difference between clicking *Update preview* and clicking *Save*: If you click *Save*, your actual site will be updated with your edits, whereas the *Update preview* button only updates the preview and leave your live website intact.

The preview of your theme, filled with default dummy content that you can't change, is the only way you can see how your changes look without saving. That's a shame, obviously, because your content might be of a kind that forces you to hit Save several times during your editing (image-heavy sites, for example). The reason Tumblr does this, though, is to show how each post type would look like on the live site.

FIGURE 9-2: Edit your theme's code from this window

Six Tips for Working with Themes

While you no doubt will figure out a workflow that works well for you, here are some pointers to help you get started while avoiding all those annoying pitfalls.

- **Use your own editor.** While it is entirely possible to do all the edits in the edit box on the customization screen, it is far from ideal. Why? First, there is no color coding for the code syntax, which makes it harder to see what's what. Tabs for making sure you easily see where an HTML tag begins and ends are also harder to work with in this box. Figure 9-3 shows my favorite code editor, Coda (available for Mac only; see http://panic.com for more), with a Tumblr theme. Compare that to the edit code box on the customization screen and the difference is clear. Obviously you'll have to copy/paste the code back and forth, but that is a small price to pay for the superior interface. Copying the code into your own editor will also give you a backup and you'll be able to undo changes if you need, which you cannot do in the Tumblr code editor.

- **Preview as much as possible.** Use the *Update preview* button in the theme code edit window frequently and study the preview to make sure your edits end up the way you want. It is better to preview often, more or less after each change, since that will make it easy for you to pinpoint what went wrong. If you have a lot of edits in and the site breaks, it is harder to figure out what broke it.

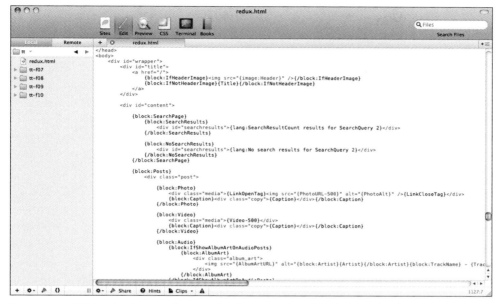

FIGURE 9-3: Editing the theme code in a code editor is preferred (Coda is used in the picture)

- **Don't click Save until it looks good.** The moment you hit Save or Save + Close, your edits will show up on the actual site. That means that you should avoid clicking Save until the preview looks good, to limit potential damage to your site's look and feel.

- **Keep a local copy.** Hey, it's the Web and things break, pages time out, and suddenly all your changes are gone. So make it a habit to keep local copies of your edited themes. My advice is to label them with the theme name, then "edit," and then the date when you backed it up. The result is along the lines of *themename-edit-2011-04-23.txt*, but with your date formatting of choice. That way you can easily take a step back in time should some edit you've made previously cause trouble.

- **Comment your edits.** As always, it is a good idea to comment your code so that you, or someone else, can figure out what it is all about. In HTML you comment code by putting it between <!-- and --> characters, whereas CSS comments belong between /* and */. You can learn more about commenting code from W3Schools: for HTML code go to `http://www.w3schools.com/tags/tag_comment.asp`; for CSS go to `http://www.w3schools.com/css/css_syntax.asp`.

- **Use a dummy site of your own.** If possible, set up a dummy site with the kind of content you intend to publish. That way you won't have to worry about clicking that *Save* button, and you can see your edits in action on a live site, rather than the preview site available on the customization screen.

How Tumblr Themes Work

Tumblr themes differ a bit from theme and template engines and solutions used by other plat-forms. First, there are no template files for various "views" or types of content, but rather every-thing sits in one master file. This includes the stylesheet, which is not the typical practice with CSS. Take a moment to check out the Redux theme, created by the Tumblr folks. To see the code, first activate the Redux theme on one of your Tumblr sites. Click Customize in the right column from your Dashboard, then click Theme in the top left. From there, click the *Use custom HTML* button and take a look at the code behind the Redux theme (refer back to Figure 9-2).

As you can see, nothing prevents you from editing the theme code right then and there (obvi-ously only for your site — you won't actually be altering the Redux theme). If you like, by all means play around a bit and use the *Update preview* button to see how it looks in the preview window with your changes. Your changes won't be saved to your site until you click *Save*. Also worth considering is that you can copy the code for a complete theme and rework it to some-thing you like. It's all there for you to play with, after all, so use that as a resource for learning.

> **TIP** While you need the customization screen with its custom HTML box to preview themes, you are usually better off copying the theme's content to your text editor of choice and working with the code there. Most decent text editors will color code the HTML and CSS markup, which makes it a lot easier to manage. Then, to preview, just copy it back to the Tumblr customization box and click Update preview to see the result.

In the code you'll find code snippets that don't look like HTML tags, residing within curly brackets much like your CSS does. These are special Tumblr tags that will output various ele-ments in your theme. A simple Tumblr tag would be "Title," which outputs the title and could be used like this (within an h1 tag):

```
<h1>{Title}</h1>
```

There are two types of Tumblr tags:

- **Variables** are placeholders for dynamic data, such as a title or description.
- **Blocks** are placeholders for blocks of data, such as all your posts, for example. Sometimes the content of a block won't be outputted; it can be conditional, meaning that some conditions needs to be met for it to be used. See the section "Under the Right Conditions" later in this chapter for more information.

Consider the code from the Redux theme again. The code mixes HTML with these Tumblr tags, and this is what powers a Tumblr site. Notice that it follows the same basic structure as any HTML page, meaning that it has a head tag, a body tag, and so on. If you have created some websites you'll no doubt recognize some techniques used for placing content with div containers and such as well.

To recap, Tumblr themes don't have a bunch of template files; instead everything resides in one master file, from CSS to HTML. Tumblr-specific tags are recognized as the ones with curly brackets around them, and through them you'll be able to place the content from your Tumblr site in the right spot, from the site title and description, to your posts, pages, and navigational links.

> You might wonder where theme images go. They are hosted on the Tumblr servers and there's an upload page at your disposal — just make sure you don't abuse it or Tumblr will ban your account. You'll learn more about this in Chapter 10; for now, you can check out the image upload page at `http://www.tumblr.com/themes/upload_static_file`. **NOTE**

More About Tumblr Tags

Tumblr has a lot of tags to help you control the output of the content in your theme, way too many to publish here. All Tumblr tags are described, along with usage and a bunch of examples, in the theme documentation (Figure 9-4), found here: `http://www.tumblr.com/docs/en/custom_themes`.

FIGURE 9-4: The Tumblr theme documentation is pretty good

Before moving on to Chapter 10 and the actual editing of Tumblr themes, you need to understand how blocks work, as well as how conditional Tumblr tags work. If you have a good grasp of HTML this will be a breeze.

As you remember, Tumblr tags sit inside curly brackets. The tag that outputs the site title looks like this, and is a variable tag, hence this is all you need for it to work:

```
<h1>{Title}</h1>
```

That would output your selected site title within h1 tags. Simple, huh? Well, blocks are a little more complicated. Just as most HTML tags need to be both opened and then closed, so do block tags. Block tags are easy to spot, with `block:` first in the name. This is the block tag for outputting the posts in the theme:

```
{block:Posts}
    THE CODE FOR THE POST OUTPUT GOES HERE
{/block:Posts}
```

You write the block tags pretty much like HTML tags that you have to close. The first one opens everything up, and you put everything needed within. Then, when done, you close it with a similar tag, but with a slash before the tag name.

You could have a block tag with other block tags within. In fact, you will since while `block:Posts` will output the post content, you probably want to style it as well, so you need to add blocks for the various types of posts, such as `block:Text` for text posts, and `block:Photo` for photo posts. It is all nested, so make sure you close the block tags within a block before closing the wrapping block.

```
{block:Posts}
    {block:Text}
        THE CODE FOR TEXT POSTS GO HERE
    {/block:Text}
    {block:Photo}
        THE CODE FOR PHOTO POSTS GO HERE
    {/block:Photo}
{/block:Posts}
```

And so on. You'll work with this more in the next chapter. Just remember that you need to both open and close block tags, just like most HTML tags.

Under the Right Conditions

Conditional tags are a way to display something (some text, an image, etc.) only if specific conditions are met. There are two kinds of conditional tags in Tumblr theming. The first kind is basically block tags that won't show up unless they are needed. The most obvious one would be `{block:Pagination}`, which is used to output the previous and next links for browsing the site. However, if there aren't any previous or next pages to show, then it won't show up.

The other kind of conditional tags are the ones related to settings. The `{block:IfHeaderImage}` tag, for example, will only be used if a header image has been uploaded, otherwise it won't show anything.

All of these tags are defined in the theme documentation (`http://www.tumblr.com/docs/en/custom_themes`). They might be a bit hard to grasp at first, which is why it is a good idea to start by looking at themes with cool features and try to figure out how those features work. So let's go play with some themes!

Picking the Right Theme to Edit

When you're picking a theme as a base, fully knowing that you'll be editing it a bit to suit your needs, you should consider its design carefully. You want to find the closest match to all your design needs because that will limit the need to edit the code. In other words, if you know you need two columns, don't go for a single column theme or you'll have to add a column yourself — it's smarter to find a two column theme and work from that.

> While the Theme Garden (`http://www.tumblr.com/themes/`) isn't the only place to find themes, it is the perfect starting point. Make sure you check it out when looking for the ideal theme! **TIP**

Knowing a bit of code is helpful when picking a theme to edit. Some changes might require only minor tweaks to the code, such as the font size for example, whereas others will require more work, as adding an extra column. Use your common sense and your coding knowledge to compare the theme you're considering with your mental image of how it should look. If they differ a lot in structure, you might be able to find a better base to build upon, whereas colors and font sizes are less of a big deal.

Finally, the more graphics a theme includes, the harder it will be to change it. While you can swap graphics (often by editing the CSS) without too much trouble, visually intense themes can make it difficult to find the appropriate visual balance. Such themes often look good because there's a balance between the visuals, so if you want to swap one graphic element out you will have to make sure that the new one works well with the rest of the graphics in the theme. One solution would be to swap out all the graphic elements, but that's quite an edit, perhaps more than you had planned? A good practice when working with graphic elements in a design is to take a screenshot of the theme and then play with different graphics in your image editing software of choice. That way you can find the balance in visuals, create the necessary images you'll need, and then make the alterations to the theme code.

> **TIP** The Print Screen (or Prt Scr) key on a Windows PC or Cmd+Shift+3 on a Mac will take screenshots of your entire desktop.

Finding Your Way in a Theme

Later in this chapter you'll edit a theme, putting things in and changing elements, but first let's take a closer look at where stuff goes by examining the Redux theme.

As I'm writing this, the Redux theme is a whopping 1127 rows of code! Most Tumblr themes are really long, which obviously is because everything sits in the same file. We won't reprint the entire theme here, but let's take a look at the major blocks.

To get the code for the Redux theme, select it on the customization screen, click the *Use custom HTML* button, and then copy the code for pasting in your favorite text editor, preferably one that lets you view line numbers.

> **NOTE** The Redux theme might have changed since this was written, so if you don't find the line mentioned on the exact line number in your version, it might have been altered or moved up or down in the line order. Try searching the theme code for the line you need. Just a heads up, since we won't be reprinting the theme here and can't link to a download file since it is the property of Tumblr.

The Declaration and Style

As with every HTML document, the theme starts with a declaration, and then the head section with tags like title, meta and such. Let's jump ahead to the Tumblr specifics, like the pretty ASCII art that says Tumblr at the top of the Redux theme, shown in Figure 9-5. This part of the code is commented out so the browser won't render it, but it certainly shows that this is a Tumblr theme, doesn't it?

```
<!DOCTYPE html PUBLIC "-//W3C//DTD XHTML 1.0 Transitional//EN" "http://www.w3.org/TR/xhtml1/DTD/xhtml1-transitional.dtd">
<!--
                     .                    .o8      oooo
       .            .o8                  "888      `888
     .o88800 oooo   oooo   ooo. .oo.  .oo.  888oooo.   888  oooo d8b
      888   `888   `888  `888P"Y88bP"Y88b  d88' `88b  888  `888""8P
      888    888    888   888   888   888  888   888  888   888
      888 .  888    888   888   888   888  888   888  888   888      .o.
     "888"  `V88V"V8P' o888o o888o o888o `Y8bod8P' o888o d888b      Y8P
-->
<html xmlns="http://www.w3.org/1999/xhtml" xml:lang="en" lang="en">
<head>
     <!-- DEFAULT VARIABLES -->
     <meta name="color:Background" content="#3b627e" />

     <meta name="font:Title" content="Arial" />
     <meta name="font:Body" content="Arial" />
     <meta name="font:Accent" content="Lucida Sans" />

     <meta name="if:Show People I Follow" content="1" />
     <meta name="if:Show Tags" content="1" />
     <meta name="if:Show Album Art on Audio Posts" content="1" />
     <meta name="if:Enable Jump Pagination" content="0" />
```

FIGURE 9-5: Look at that pretty ASCII art at the top of the Redux theme (screenshot taken in the Coda editor)

The first part of the code we want to explore is the section marked DEFAULT VARIABLES, beginning on line 15 and continuing to 30, and sporting a bunch of meta tags.

```
<!-- DEFAULT VARIABLES -->
<meta name="color:Background" content="#3b627e" />

<meta name="font:Title" content="Arial" />
<meta name="font:Body" content="Arial" />
<meta name="font:Accent" content="Lucida Sans" />

<meta name="if:Show People I Follow" content="1" />
<meta name="if:Show Tags" content="1" />
<meta name="if:Show Album Art on Audio Posts" content="1" />
<meta name="if:Enable Jump Pagination" content="0" />

<meta name="text:Disqus Shortname" content="" />

<meta name="image:Header" content="" />
<meta name="image:Background" content="" />
```

What are those tags? The meta tag is obviously HTML, but what do the name="" parts mean? Well, those meta tags are what's creating the settings for the theme. The first actual line of code says that the background has a default value of #3b627e, which of course is a color. I figure this out because within the meta tag the name says color:Background, and the content is the #3b627e color. The next line with code has the name font:Title and content that says Arial, so that's the font for the site title, defaulting to Arial.

Now look at the theme settings for the Redux theme (shown in Figure 9-6), found under Appearance on the customization screen, showing options corresponding to these meta tags.

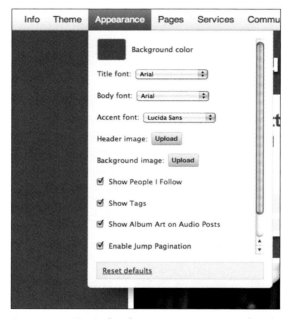

FIGURE 9-6: The Redux theme settings correspond to the meta tags in the theme code

There are a bunch of options for doing interesting stuff with meta tags and such, all documented in the theme documentation: `http://www.tumblr.com/docs/en/custom_themes`.

Moving on, you see some basic HTML code, littered with Tumblr tags such as `{Title}` and `{block:Description}`. The theme documentation at the aforementioned URL provides details on specific Tumblr tags.

The next line of interest is line 38, where we first encounter the opening style tag:

```
<style type="text/css">
```

Everything from this line down to line 782, which closes the style tag, is the CSS. This part of the code controls how things look, how big the elements will be, what font is used, and so on. This is where you write the actual design of the HTML markup that follows.

After that, from line 783 to 842, you'll find some CSS tailored for Internet Explorer and its quirks when it comes to showing CSS. If you look at these lines in a code editor you'll most likely see them commented out. That's because only Internet Explorer will read them.

Line 843 is a bit interesting:

```
<style type="text/css">{CustomCSS}</style>
```

This is another style block, but it consists only of the {CustomCSS} Tumblr tag. The {CustomCSS} tag will output what you have entered in the Add custom CSS box, located on the Advanced tab for your theme's settings (see Figure 9-7). Since the {CustomCSS} is placed after the original CSS (between line 38 and 782), it will overwrite the CSS set previously, assuming you have actually put any CSS code in the Add custom CSS box. This feature can be very useful if you need to edit some CSS quickly but don't want to fiddle with over 700 lines of CSS.

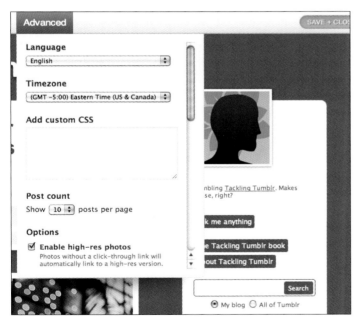

FIGURE 9-7: Add custom CSS from the box on the Advanced tab to alter the CSS of a theme without messing with the code

That does it for the top of the theme code. Next is the actual content.

NOTE   While you can overwrite CSS rules with custom code, remember that the original CSS will be read by the web browser, and then your custom CSS will load. This is great for minor changes, but if you need to make a lot of changes to the CSS you are better off editing the actual CSS than overwriting it. It is considered best practice not to overwrite too many rules, and the less code the web browser has to load, the fast the site will show up on the reader's screen.

The Content

As with all HTML sites, you'll find the actual content that the web browser outputs between the body tags. Tumblr themes are no different, so from line 847, where the body tags starts, to the second to last line you'll find the HTML and Tumblr tags that output the content. Most of this is pretty straightforward, with div containers where the content sits, positioned and styled by the CSS from the head section.

Basically, the Redux theme has the following HTML structure within the body tag:

```
<div id="wrapper">
    <div id="title">
        CODE FOR OUTPUTTING THE TITLE
    </div>
    <div id="content">
        THE SITE CONTENT, FOOTER AND NAVIGATION
    </div>
    <div id="sidebar">
        THE RIGHT COLUMN
    </div>
</div>
```

This is somewhat simplified but it is the major layout of the Redux theme, so if you get lost you can use this as a reference.

Take a look at the div#title (the div with id="title") and the code within. It spans lines 847-852 in the Redux theme:

```
<div id="title">
    <a href="/">
        {block:IfHeaderImage}
          <img src="{image:Header}" />
        {/block:IfHeaderImage}
        {block:IfNotHeaderImage}{Title}{/block:IfNotHeaderImage}
    </a>
</div>
```

You see some Tumblr tags here, including two conditional tags. First is `{block:IfHeaderImage}`, which checks whether there is a header image uploaded for the theme. If so, it will output everything up to its closing tag, `{/block:IfHeaderImage}`. In this case that's an `img` (image) tag containing the chosen image, which is fetched by the Tumblr tag `{image:Header}`.

If there isn't a header image available then the `{block:IfNotHeaderImage}` Tumblr tag is true, and hence everything between it and its closing tag, `{/block:IfNotHeaderImage}`, will be outputted. That is just the site title, via the Tumblr tag `{Title}`.

That's really all there is to the Redux theme, and just about any other Tumblr theme. They can differ in layout and design as well as Tumblr tag usage, but because everything sits in the same file this is how the code will look.

> Having a hard time getting an overview of the Tumblr theme you're working with? Start by locating the major wrapping div containers, such as the main content, the header and possibly footer, along with any side column there might be. And again, use a code editor. This will give you color syntax, which makes it a lot easier to see where everything goes and what it is. A colorizing code editor is your best tool for navigating any Tumblr theme code.
>
> **TIP**

Theme Editing Exercises

Enough theory; it's time to practice your theme editing skills. The following examples will guide you through a variety of edits to several free Tumblr themes.

First, here are a few terms you need to know:

- `div#header` means the div container (an HTML tag) with the `id="header"`.
- `div.post` means the div container with the `class="post"`.
- Text within curly brackets are Tumblr tags, for example, `{Title}`.

So when you read "You'll find `{Title}` in `div#header` and the actual content in any of the `div.post` tags," that means that the Tumblr tag `{Title}` is located in the div with `id="header"`, and the mentioned content is in any div with `class="post"`.

Revisiting the Facebook Fan Page Widget

Remember the Facebook fan page widget from Chapter 8? Great, then you already know how to add a Facebook widget to your sidebar using the Description box. But what if you want to put that widget someplace else, say at the bottom of the page? In those cases you will have to edit the theme code to add the box where you want it.

In this example I'll add my fan page box to a Tumblr blog I have, which you can find on `http://tdhftw.tumblr.com.`, using the Manuscript Neue theme which is available for free on Tumblr. As Figure 9-8 shows, there's no side column to play with in this theme, so I'll add the box at the bottom, on each page. You can follow along on your own Tumblr site if you like. Feel free to add my fan page box there, although I recommend using a Facebook box (any type of like box really) tailored to your fan page, or your Facebook user: `http://developers.facebook.com/docs/plugins/.`

FIGURE 9-8: No sidebar for the fan page box on http://tdhftw.tumblr.com (using the Manuscript Neue theme)

In this example, I want to add the Facebook fan page box right after the stream of posts and before the pagination. Figure 9-9 illustrates the desired outcome.

FIGURE 9-9: This is where I want the fan page box

The active width of the content is 500 pixels in this theme, so the Facebook box will need to have the same width. There's room a wider box, but it'll look better if it is the same width as the actual content. I found out the width by viewing the source code on `http://tdhftw.tumblr.com`. The content is in `ol#posts`, which is 580 pixels wide, and every containing `li.post` has a margin-left of 80 pixels, which leaves 500 pixels of actual width to use. If you're using a decent web browser, you can use extensions or built-in web developer tools to "inspect" elements in a web page, eliminating the need for such backtracking. How you use these features depends on your web browser; for example, Firefox works best if you have the Firebug extension (`http://getfirebug.com`), while Safari and Chrome have the feature built into the right-click contextual menu. Refer to the web browser's documentation for details.

So the fan page box should be 500 pixels. At `http://developers.facebook.com/docs/reference/plugins/like-box/` I enter that value, along with some other settings for the box. I'm also cutting both the stream and the header for the Facebook box by unchecking the appropriate boxes on the Facebook page. Click the *Get code* button to display the code (see Figure 9-10), and copy it.

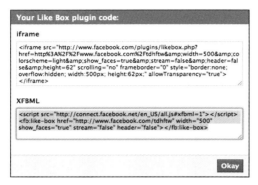

I'll paste the following code into the Tumblr theme code to get my fan page box up:

```
<script src="http://connect.facebook.net/en_US/all.js#xfbml=1"></
  script><fb:like-box href="http://www.facebook.com/tdhftw"
  width="500" show_faces="true" stream="false" header="false"></
  fb:like-box>
```

The next step is finding the right place in the theme code. Begin on the customization screen, and click the *Custom HTML* button under Theme to make the theme's code show in the Custom HTML box. Make sure you pick the Manuscript Neue theme first to get the right code.

Notice that this theme consists of a lot fewer lines than the Redux theme. (In fact, it is only about half the length of the Redux theme.) I want to add the Facebook box at the bottom, just before the page navigation links, so I scroll way down, in fact almost all the way. On line 603 you'll find this code, which tells you that the `{block:Posts}` Tumblr tag ends here, along with the `ol` tag in which all the content is listed, one `li` at the time.

```
{/block:Posts}</ol>
```

Below that, on lines 605-609, is the pagination block, which I want to have directly after the Facebook fan box:

```
{block:Pagination}<div id="pagination">
    {block:PreviousPage}<a href="{PreviousPage}"
      class="previous">&larr; Previous Posts</a>
```

```
    {/block:PreviousPage}

    {block:NextPage}<a href="{NextPage}" class="next">
      Next Posts &rarr;</a>{/block:NextPage}
</div>{/block:Pagination}
```

I could just insert a div container for the Facebook fan box between the `{/block:Posts}` and the `{block:Pagination}` tags, but I want to keep this simple and don't want to write a bunch of new CSS, so I'll just sneak it in as a `li` within the `ol`, but after the `{/block:Posts}` tag since I don't want it to be within the Tumblr content loop. `{block:Posts}` is the tag that outputs the content; you can read more about it in the theme documentation at `http://www.tumblr.com/docs/en/custom_themes#posts`.

This is the result, a spanking new `li` item before the closing of the `ol` tag:

```
    {/block:Posts}
    <li>
        <!-- MY FACEBOOK FAN BOX -->
        <script
          src="http://connect.facebook.net/en_US/all.js#xfbml=1
          "></script><fb:like-box
          href="http://www.facebook.com/tdhftw" width="500"
          show_faces="true" stream="false"
          header="false"></fb:like-box>
    </li>
</ol>
```

Click *Update preview* to see the changes. As Figure 9-11 shows, it's not a direct hit, with the box being too far to the left and too tight to the pagination part below.

A quick look in the CSS code at the top of the document, lines 292-294, tells me that the class `.post` will fix that problem:

```
.post {
    margin-left: 80px;
}
```

FIGURE 9-11: The edited theme still needs work

Adding `class="post"` to the `li` containing the Facebook fan page will give it the same treatment as the posts, in terms of margin to the left at least:

```
{/block:Posts}
<li class="post">
    <!-- MY FACEBOOK FAN BOX -->
    <script
      src=http://connect.facebook.net/en_US/all.js#xfbml=1
    ></script><fb:like-box
    href="http://www.facebook.com/tdhftw" width="500"
    show_faces="true" stream="false"
    header="false"></fb:like-box>
</li>
</ol>
```

Click *Update preview* again to see the changes. Hey, look, now it is centered, as shown in Figure 9-12!

Suspendisse ac pede. Cras tincidunt pretium felis. Cum sociis natoque
penatibus et magnis dis parturient montes, nascetur ridiculus mus.
Pellentesque porttitor mi id felis. Maecenas nec augue. Praesent a quam
pretium leo congue accumsan.

TDH on Facebook

317 people like TDH.

Theme = Manuscript Neue

FIGURE 9-12: The box in the right place

That's better, but I still need some more space below the box. A quick look at some other posts shows that this is something that `div.meta` usually does, adding a margin-bottom of 50 pixels to the `li` the box sits in. I don't need any metadata — things like how many notes there are and when the post was published — because this `li` doesn't contain a post but just the Facebook fan page box. What I need is to give the Facebook box `li` a margin-bottom of 50 pixels; that should sort it out. I'll cheat a bit and do it with the style tag in the `li` just to see how it looks:

```
{/block:Posts}
<li class="post" style="margin-bottom: 50px;">
    <!-- MY FACEBOOK FAN BOX -->
    <script
      src="http://connect.facebook.net/en_US/all.js#xfbml=1
      "></script><fb:like-box
      href="http://www.facebook.com/tdhftw" width="500"
      show_faces="true" stream="false"
      header="false"></fb:like-box>
    </li>
</ol>
```

Figure 9-13 shows that edit worked perfectly! Now I'm happy with the box, but less happy with the style solution. Hardcoding CSS into a tag isn't something I condone, but then again everything sits in this file and it isn't used anywhere else, so maybe it is OK.

FIGURE 9-13: The Facebook fan page box where it should be

No, I don't like it: it is not considered best practice to use inline style like this. As an alternative approach, I'll add a class, called `.tdh-fb`, to the `li` with the box, and remove the style part altogether. The Facebook box part now looks like this:

```
{/block:Posts}
<li class="post tdh-fb">
    <!-- MY FACEBOOK FAN BOX -->
    <script
      src="http://connect.facebook.net/en_US/all.js#xfbml=1
      "></script><fb:like-box
      href="http://www.facebook.com/tdhftw" width="500"
      show_faces="true" stream="false"
      header="false"></fb:like-box>
</li>
</ol>
```

You can have any number of IDs and classes in an HTML tag; just separate them with a space. In this case the classes `.post` and `.tdh-fb` are in the `li`.

Now I need to add the margin-bottom: 50px part to the `.tdh-fb` class. That CSS rule belongs up in the style tag in the head section way up in the document. I'll add it just after the `.post` part, which you'll find on lines 292-294, pretty early in the code, but I could add it just about anywhere as long as it is within the style tag.

There's another option as well: adding the CSS rules in the *Add custom CSS* box under the Advanced tab, as shown earlier in Figure 9-6. To me this doesn't make as much sense in this example because I'm already fiddling with the theme code, but if all my alterations had been CSS edits it would be fine.

There is an even better choice than adding the Facebook box in a li, as I've done in this example. A li is a list item in an ol (ordered list), and while the posts outputted are parts of that list, the box really isn't. That means that it would be more semantically correct to put the Facebook box in a div, after the closing `</ol>` tag but before the `{block:Pagination}` tag. So why didn't I? Two reasons: First, a lot of themes are built around ol lists, and the simplest solution by far is just to add additional li tags to them, so I wanted to show that. Second, if you add the Facebook box to a div after the closing ol, you'll have to alter the stylesheet for the ol and possibly its final li to make sure the div with the Facebook box doesn't end up too far below the last post (being the last li) outputted. Also, you would need to style the Facebook div to behave as a li to get it to look good. It is a larger edit to the theme, and that means it is more difficult for those of you who are less HTML-savvy. We'll play more by the semantic rules in Chapter 10, when we build a theme.

IMPORTANT

Adding Disqus to Non-Ready Themes

Not all themes are ready for Disqus, the hosted commenting solution. The ones that are have a box in which you put your Disqus shortname for the site in question, as detailed in Chapter 7. However, there's nothing stopping you from adding Disqus to any theme, and it is a fairly easy task, outlined in the following steps. Obviously you should only do this on a theme that is not Disqus ready, so look for any theme that catches your eye that doesn't have that Disqus shortlink box described in Chapter 7.

1. If you haven't already done so, sign up for Disqus and create your site on that service. Refer to Chapter 7 if you're unfamiliar with Disqus or need further help.

2. Log in to Disqus, go to Install and choose Tumblr in the left menu. You will be directed to the page with the installation instructions. (You can also use this direct link: `http://disqus.com/admin/tumblr/`.) Scroll down to the advanced instructions, shown in Figure 9-14.

   You must be logged in and have a site set up to view this screen. If you have more than one site, make sure you have selected the site you want to be working with on Disqus. Otherwise the codes on this page will be the wrong ones.

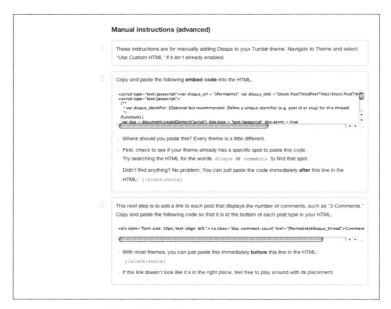

FIGURE 9-14: The advanced installation instructions on Disqus
Copyright 2007-2011 · DISQUS

3. The Disqus website explains the three easy steps (shown in Figure 9-14) to add the Disqus code.

    a. Go to the customization screen for your Tumblr site, and click *Use custom HTML* under Theme. Some themes are prepared for Disqus in the design, but lack that fancy little box for your site's shortname, which you'll no doubt remember from Chapter 7, or the Redux theme for that matter.

    b. It is worth looking through the code for comments or div containers that are named comments, `disqus` or similar. If you find one, copy the code from step 2 on the Disqus page and paste it in the container.

    Should you not find the appropriate divs, look for `{/block:Posts}`, which is the Tumblr tag for closing the content loop. (You saw this tag in the Facebook fan box example previously.) Copy the code from step 2 on the Disqus page and paste it after `{/block:Posts}`.

    Don't forget that there are settings for the Disqus box' appearance on Disqus; see Chapter 7 for more on this.

If the Disqus comments don't line up the way you want on your site, you can use CSS to make things work better. The whole Disqus comment block sits in a div called `div#disqus_thread`, and you can get to individual elements within it. Just study the source code on your site and add the necessary CSS to the `style` element in your theme's header.

TIP

---

c. Step 3 on the Disqus install page for Tumblr contains the code needed for showing the comment count, and linking it to the comments. Because Tumblr doesn't support comments out of the box you will want to add the code to the content flow. This is the suggested code from Disqus:

```
<div style="font-size: 10px; text-align: left;">
  <a class="dsq-comment-count"
    href="{Permalink}#disqus_thread">Comments</a>
  </div>
```

You can alter the code if you'd like, to change the font size, for example.

Where you place this all depends on your theme. Disqus suggest placing the code before the `{/block:Posts}` tag, which works fine but might not fit your theme's design. A lot of themes have div containers for metadata (date posted, notes and so on), so you might want to look for those divs. (Recall `div.meta` from the Facebook example earlier in the chapter? That is obviously where the comment count should go if you want to add Disqus commenting to the theme you have chosen.)

That's all there is to it, really. Now you can add Disqus to any Tumblr theme.

Adding an Ask Box Anywhere

Are you addicted to the Ask feature, or just want to promote it more? While enabling the feature gives you an /ask page to link, you can actually embed the Ask box anywhere, much like you embed a YouTube movie. You might want it in your sidebar all the time, at the top or bottom of your posts, or someplace else.

The code for embedding the Ask box is simple and has been circulating online for a while:

```
<iframe frameborder="0" scrolling="no" width="100%" height="149"
  src="http://www.tumblr.com/ask_form/yoursite.tumblr.com"
  style="background-color:transparent; overflow:hidden;"
  id="ask_form"></iframe>
<!--[if IE]>
  <script type="text/javascript">
```

```
document.getElementById('ask_form').allowTransparency=true;
</script>
<![endif]-->
```

Be sure to replace `yoursite` in the `src` for the iframe tag with your own sitename.

That's it. Paste the code wherever it fits in your theme, as in the Facebook fan box example earlier in this chapter.

You can even paste it in a post. To do so, you have to click the *HTML* button in the text editor on the Write Text post screen, because pasting the code in the WYSIWYG editor won't work. Figure 9-15 shows the result. A fancy way of giving your Asks a bit more exposure, wouldn't you say?

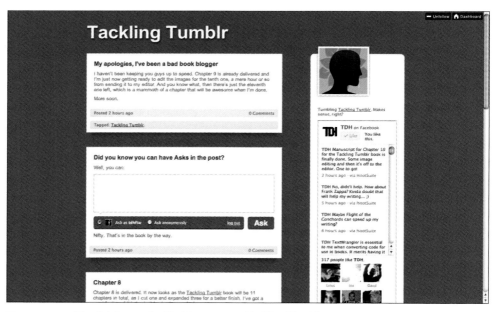

FIGURE 9-15: The Ask box embedded in a post on Tackling Tumblr

Enhancing SEO on Your Tumblr Sites

Tumblr isn't exactly known for great search engine optimization (SEO). Good SEO helps search engines like Google or Bing find your content. You can edit your theme to make it easier for the search engines, and thus potential readers, to find your site.

SEO isn't an exact science and there are a lot of theories about what makes for good SEO practices. It doesn't help that the search engines tweak their search methods all the time. Do what you can to strengthen your site's SEO, and keep up with the changes by reading blogs on the matter if you like, but don't rely or pay good money for an universal solution for owning every search on Google. It's never that easy. Good content and lots of links for it is the best way to go.

NOTE

You can make a few edits to help search engines find your content. Start with the title tag, found in head. This is one of the tags that tell search engines what the page is all about. The title tag should contain the title of your site, but also something about the actual content. The following code is a suggestion as to what you could put in the title tag, starting with a summary of the post, should there be one, and then the site's title itself.

```
<title>{block:PostSummary}{PostSummary} - {/block:PostSummary}
  {Title}</title>
```

Why not use `{PostTitle}` instead? Well, that tag won't return anything for posts without a title, which is just about everything that isn't a text post. The `{PostSummary}` tag outputs the same thing as `{PostTitle}` if there is a title for the post, but if there isn't, it outputs a summary of the content instead.

While you're at it, why not improve the meta tags in head as well?

```
<meta name="title" content="{block:PostSummary}{PostSummary} - {/
  block:PostSummary}{Title}">
<meta name="description" content="{block:PostSummary}{PostSummary}
  - {/block:PostSummary}{Title} - {Description}">
<meta name="keywords" content="{block:Permalink}{block:Posts}
  {block:Tags}{Tag}, {/block:Tags}{/block:Posts}{/
  block:Permalink}">
```

Same thing here, obviously, with the addition of `{Description}` to the meta tag for descriptions. The meta tag for keywords relies primarily on the tags you've chosen for your post, using `{Tag}` to get them. This means that relevant tagging of posts results in the same tags in the meta HTML tag, which can help.

Proper headings are also important. For example, the title of the site on your site's front page is the most important thing, so that should be within an h1 tag. However, when reading an actual post the post title is more important, so the site heading shouldn't be h1, but rather h2. You can manage that with this little code snippet, ready for use in your theme. If you're having trouble finding the particular block in your theme, copy the theme code to a text editor on your computer and do a search for `{block:IndexPage}`.

```
{block:IndexPage}
    <h1 class="site-title">
        <a href="/">{Title}</a>
    </h1>
{/block:IndexPage}
{block:PermalinkPage}
    <h2 class="site-title">
        <a href="/">{Title}</a>
    </h2>
{/block:PermalinkPage}
```

Depending on where on the site you are you'll get a different result. On the front page you'll get the h1, thanks to the Tumblr tag {block:IndexPage}, and on post pages you'll get the h2 with the use of {block:PermalinkPage}. Notice that both the h1 and the h2 have the .site-title class; this is so you can style them both exactly the same, despite being two different tags.

```
.site-title {
    font-size: 36px;
    border-bottom: 1px solid #ff0000;
}
```

Obviously you'll need to alter the headings for your posts as well. On the front page, and any page that is listing content, you'll want them to be h2 (since the site title is h1), but on single post pages you'll want them to be h1 (where the site title is h2). This is just as easily done using the following code:

```
{block:Title}
    {block:IndexPage}
        <h2>
            <a href="{Permalink}">{Title}</a>
        </h2>
    {/block:IndexPage}
    {block:PermalinkPage}
        <h1>
            {Title}
        </h1>
    {/block:PermalinkPage}
{/block:Title}
```

This is the same procedure as with the site title, with the difference that the whole thing sits inside the `{block:Title}` because that's where the post title goes. Also, notice that the h2 version, for listings, contains a link to the post (with `{Permalink}` in an a tag) whereas the post title is unlinked on single post pages. After all, why link the post when you're already there?

What more can you do to improve your search potential? The following suggestions aren't theme edits, but they can help your content's ranking in search engines:

- **Pick dedicated URL slugs.** By choosing the URL for your post, and making sure that the most important keywords are in the slug, you'll make it easier for search engines to find your content.

- **Get links for your content from other sites.** Best of all is if the keyword for your post is linked, so if you've got a great post on tomatoes, then getting a link from another site where the linked word is "tomatoes" is smart.

- **Make sure your site validates.** The theme you're running should validate in `http://validator.w3.org`; search engines like that.

All in all, great content is usually rewarded, and the more links you get the better.

> Did you know your Tumblr site has a sitemap that you can submit to Google and other search engines? You'll find it at `http://yoursite.tumblr.com/sitemap.xml` (replace `yoursite` with your site name, of course). Visit the major search engines and find their submission pages for sitemaps for better indexing of your site.   **TIP**

Summary

Now you know a little bit more about working with the theme code. You should be confident enough to make your own edits and tweak themes to meet your needs. After all, if you can find the element you want to change, you can alter it, using additional HTML code or by editing the CSS.

The logical next, and final, step is to create a theme of your own. That's coming in Chapter 10.

chapter 10
Your Own Tumblr Theme

in this chapter

- How to get started with a Tumblr theme
- Creating a brand new theme
- Submitting and selling your theme

WHAT BETTER WAY to learn more about creating Tumblr themes than to actually create one? This chapter walks you through building a fairly simple yet complete Tumblr theme that you can modify to fit your needs. First, you'll think about how to get started when you want to create a new theme. You'll build the theme bit by bit, and finally, you'll learn how you can submit and/or sell your theme.

NOTE	This is a pretty code-intensive chapter, so if you feel that your knowledge of HTML and CSS isn't quite good enough, try to learn more. You can find more resources in Appendix A.

Getting Started with a Theme

To start the creation process of a new Tumblr theme you need at least a general idea of what you want. Sometimes the idea will be visual, and you'll create multiple mockups in Photoshop or some other image processor; at other times you may have just a basic layout that you want to work from.

In this chapter you'll build a theme. The idea is to make something that can be easily customized for different types of usage. Because you'll be building it from scratch, more or less, you'll know its ins and outs and hence it'll be easy to edit it the way you want.

The plan is to build a theme framework for you to work from. For the example in this chapter, the theme will meet the following criteria:

- It will be centered.
- It will support all of Tumblr's post formats.
- It will have a flexible top area for logos and menus.
- It will have a footer area that can be easily styled, in case you want to connect the header and footer in some fashion.
- It will have two column with a fixed width layout.
- It will support Disqus comments from the start.
- It will have a clean design so that it works out of the box.
- The theme code will validate.
- The theme code will be relatively simple and straightforward.

But I Want to Build a Theme From My Own Design!

If you want to generate a theme from your own design, then you should! The criteria I have outlined are meant to make something you can work on, and to keep it fairly simple. However, if you have created a design that you want to use as a basis for a theme, the process could go something like this:

1. Do a sketch on paper, if that's your sort of thing. It usually helps with the second step, but not all people need or want to do this.

2. Create the design in your favorite image processor. It is a good idea to make sure you can pull various elements such as logos or other graphics from the design. Use an image processor that features layers, and put those to good use for the best result.

3. Write the HTML and CSS, meaning that you'll actually create an HTML page that looks like your design. Be sure to validate the code, and have it feature every type of post format that you want to support.

4. Create a Tumblr theme of your HTML file by adding the Tumblr tags and tweaking the HTML file.

5. Add the additional features you want, such as Disqus or custom CSS support.

Getting the Graphics Right

There are two factors to consider when it comes to graphic elements in your design. First, do you want them to be interchangeable? This mainly applies to elements such as site logos and backgrounds, and is handled with Tumblr tags such as `{image:Logo}` or `{image:Background}`. We'll use those tags in the example theme in this chapter.

Second, do you want to host your images on an external server or with Tumblr? I recommend hosting the images with Tumblr for a couple of reasons. Having the images hosted externally will most likely slow down your site, and it creates vulnerability because if the image host goes down, your images will be broken and your Tumblr site will look bad.

To host your images with Tumblr, upload them using the link at `http://www.tumblr.com/themes/upload_static_file` (as shown in Figure 10-1).

FIGURE 10-1: The upload page for theme graphics

This is where you upload static files to Tumblr. This is allowed only when you're creating a theme. Tumblr notifies you that your account will be suspended if you abuse this service.

> **NOTE** To submit your theme to Tumblr's Theme Garden you have to host all external resources, including images, with Tumblr using the uploader.

About the File Formats

Traditionally, three file formats are used for images on the Web:

- GIF
- JPG (or JPEG)
- PNG

GIF format has a maximum of 256 colors and supports transparency. *Transparency* means that it can contain parts of the image that are "empty," meaning that the background would seep through. The fact that GIF format only supports up to 256 colors means that GIF is poorly suited for photos or other color-rich motifs. GIFs can be animated, as you no doubt have seen on Tumblr already.

JPG files can contain millions of colors and are suited for photos and other color-intensive motifs. When you create a JPG file in an image processor you're usually (depending on the software) able to set the compression of the file. The tighter you compress it, the less disk space it will require and the faster it'll load. However, compression degrades the quality, which means that a heavily compressed JPG usually looks bad. Use the image processor's preview feature to see how much you can compress each image, since the smaller the better.

PNG files are something of a mix of GIF and JPG. There are 8-bit PNG files that support only 256 colors, and 24-bit PNG files that can have millions of colors. PNG files, though, aren't as kind to disk space (and hence download times) as JPG files are, which means that a PNG version of a photo is huge and takes a lot of time to download, but it looks good. There is limited support for the PNG format in older web browsers (such as Internet Explorer 6 and 7, for example), but all modern ones handle it well. PNG supports transparency, as GIF does, but offers a skilled graphic designer more choice on the matter, making the format a better choice in most cases.

For the example theme in this chapter, how you create your images for your theme and what file format you rely on is entirely up to you. Use your image processor and play around; then use whatever save/export for web feature your processor has. When saving for the Web, you'll often get a preview overview of various settings as well as the chance to compare file size (see Figure 10-2).

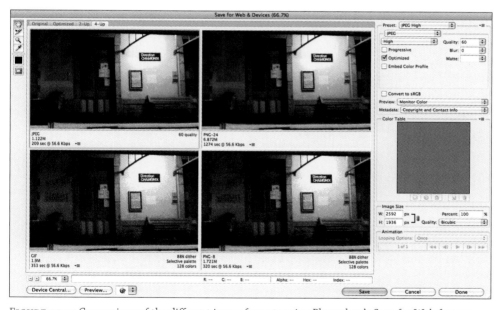

FIGURE 10-2: Comparison of the different image formats using Photoshop's Save for Web feature

Building the Theme

Now that the details are out of the way it is time to start building the theme. The main steps in the process are:

1. Create sketch and mockup.

2. Create the HTML structure.

3. Style the HTML with CSS.

4. Add the Tumblr tags to make it an actual theme.

5. Add the custom features.

Let's get started!

A Quick Sketch

I'm a big fan of doing sketches by hand; the process helps me think. For this theme there really isn't that much to sketch but I created a sketch anyway, adding some notes on the various div containers that the end code will need. Obviously this is the coder in me thinking ahead. Figure 10-3 shows the sketch from my trusty notebook.

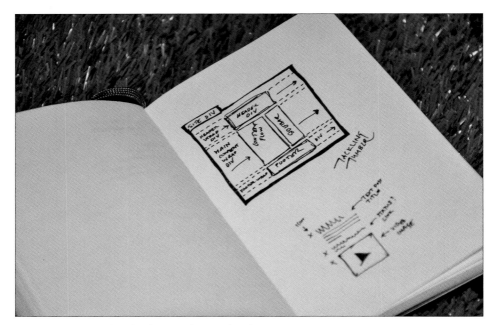

FIGURE 10-3: The old school pen and paper sketch

It is often a good idea to do a mockup on your computer as well. Image processors like Photoshop (available for Windows and Mac; `http://www.adobe.com/products/photoshopfamily.html`), Pixelmator (Mac only; `http://www.pixelmator.com`) or The Gimp (Linux, Windows, and Mac; `http://www.gimp.org`) are great tools for this.

Figure 10-4 shows a simple mockup of the theme design. I have added some dummy content to illustrate how the content flow should look per default. It might interest you to know that the icons come from the very cool `http://thenounproject.com`.

FIGURE 10-4: Theme design mockup made in Photoshop

Building the HTML

It is usually a good idea to start by writing the actual HTML code, so that is the next step. Then you'll add the look and feel with CSS. The fact that you're keeping CSS out of the code for now means that the result after the HTML is written will look bad. That's okay; this is the structure, design comes next.

The Main Structure

Consulting the sketches, you can see this is a pretty simple two-column design. You have a header area at the top where the title goes, then the main content to the left, a side column to the right, and you need some sort of footer to tie the whole thing up at the bottom.

Here is the basic HTML code for this setup:

```
<!DOCTYPE html PUBLIC "-//W3C//DTD XHTML 1.0 Transitional//EN"
  "http://www.w3.org/TR/xhtml1/DTD/xhtml1-transitional.dtd">
<html xmlns="http://www.w3.org/1999/xhtml" xml:lang="en"
  lang="en">
<head>
    <title>Site Title</title>
</head>
<body>
    <div id="site">
        <div id="header-wrap">
            <div id="header">
                <h1 class="site-title">Site Title</h1>
            </div>
        </div>
        <div id="main-wrap">
            <!-- CONTENT COLUMN -->
            <div id="content">
                <!-- Posts go here -->
            </div>
            <!-- SIDE COLUMN -->
            <div id="sidebar">
                <!-- Side column content -->
            </div>
        </div>
        <!-- THE FOOTER -->
        <div id="footer-wrap">
            <div id="footer">
                <!-- Footer content -->
            </div>
        </div>
    </div>
</body>
</html>
```

So why the wrapping div containers? Well, the idea is that it should be easy to add style to the header, with the option to stretch it visually across the full screen if you'd want to. As the sketches show, the site is centered and pretty tight, but perhaps you want to give the top and bottom of the site their own backgrounds. That's easily done by applying CSS to div#header-wrap and div#footer-wrap, both of which will fill the browser window from side to side.

Now that you have the structure, you can get the markup for the actual content in there. Doing that now will speed up the process when you add the Tumblr template tags.

The Posts

The actual posts go within the `div#content` container, under the CONTENT COLUMN comment in the code, since that is where you'll be displaying it. Here's the text post HTML:

```
<div class="post text">
    <h2>
        <a href="">The Text Post Title</a>
    </h2>
    <div class="text-content">
        <p>The text post content.</p>
        <p>Will be several p tags.</p>
        <p>And so on...</p>
    </div>
    <div class="postmeta">
        <div class="postmeta-time">
            The timestamp
        </div>
        <div class="postmeta-like">
            The number of likes
        </div>
    </div>
</div>
```

Nothing too complicated there; just some div containers with classes (since you could have several posts based on this markup per page, meaning that you can't use IDs), and the proper markup for the text posts. Notice that the wrapping div carries two classes, `post` and `text`. There are some global style elements such as margins that will apply to all posts, and you can save time by applying the `post` class to all post container divs.

Photo posts will look the same as video posts but with a different icon. Here's the HTML code:

```
<div class="post photo">
    <div class="photo-content">
        <div class="photo-img">
            <img src="photo.jpg" />
        </div>
        <p>A possible caption goes here</p>
    </div>
```

```
    <div class="postmeta">
        <div class="postmeta-time">
            The timestamp
        </div>
        <div class="postmeta-like">
            The number of likes
        </div>
    </div>
</div>
```

There's the post class in the wrapping div again. Moving on to quote posts (yes, I'm doing this in the order of the icons from the Tumblr Dashboard):

```
<div class="post quote">
    <div class="quote-content">
        <h2>The quote goes here</h2>
        <p class="quote-source">Who said it?</p>
    </div>
    <div class="postmeta">
        <div class="postmeta-time">
            The timestamp
        </div>
        <div class="postmeta-like">
            The number of likes
        </div>
    </div>
</div>
```

In addition to styling the actual quote, let's also style its source in case that's submitted. Still, pretty straightforward. By now you've noticed that the div.postmeta is in every one of these code markups. This is just for the HTML version; you won't have to repeat it when you apply the actual Tumblr tags. We'll get to that later.

Here's the link HTML markup:

```
<div class="post link">
    <div class="link-content">
        <h2>
            <a href="">Here's the link text</a>
        </h2>
        <p>Possible description of the link.</p>
    </div>
```

```
<div class="postmeta">
    <div class="postmeta-time">
        The timestamp
    </div>
    <div class="postmeta-like">
        The number of likes
    </div>
</div>
</div>
```

Looks familiar right? Link posts are obviously linked, so that's why you need the link tag around the link text, much like the title for the text post.

Chat is next. This block makes less sense without the Tumblr tags to alter the code, but none-theless, here's the markup:

```
<div class="post chat">
    <h2>
        <a href="">The Chat Post Title</a>
    </h2>
    <div class="chat-content">
        <div class="chat-lines">
            <div class="line odd">
                <strong>Mike</strong> Hi Dave!
            </div>
            <div class="line even">
                <strong>Dave</strong> Mike! How goes it?
            </div>
            <div class="line odd">
                <strong>Mike</strong> Great man!
            </div>
            <div class="line even">
                <strong>Dave</strong> OK, CYA!
            </div>
        </div>
    </div>
    <div class="postmeta">
        <div class="postmeta-time">
            The timestamp
        </div>
        <div class="postmeta-like">
            The number of likes
```

```
            </div>
        </div>
</div>
```

Each line in the chat gets its own div container, but every other line also gets the class `alt` to display a different background.

Here's the HTML markup for audio posts:

```
<div class="post audio">
    <div class="audio-content">
        <div class="audio-album">
            <img src="album.jpg" />
        </div>
        <div class="audio-player">
            <!-- Code for the player -->
        </div>
        <div class="audio-player-meta">
            Download
        </div>
    </div>
    <div class="postmeta">
        <div class="postmeta-time">
            The timestamp
        </div>
        <div class="postmeta-like">
            The number of likes
        </div>
    </div>
</div>
```

Sometimes Tumblr can find the album artwork for your audio clip, so you need to include code to display it appropriately. Also, the player that actually makes it possible to listen to the audio from your site needs to have a spot, along with the download file link. All and all, still pretty straightforward.

The final post format is video. Take a look at the code:

```
<div class="post video">
    <div class="video-content">
        <div class="video-player">
            <!-- Video embed goes here -->
```

```
        </div>
        <p>A possible caption goes here</p>
    </div>
    <div class="postmeta">
        <div class="postmeta-time">
            The timestamp
        </div>
        <div class="postmeta-like">
            The number of likes
        </div>
    </div>
</div>
```

As you can see it is all but identical to photo posts, with the difference that you won't display an image but the embed code for the video itself.

You're almost done with the post content! One item remains; if the Ask feature is enabled, you need HTML for how Ask posts should look when they show up in the content flow. So here's the markup for Ask posts:

```
<div class="post ask">
    <div class="ask-content">
        <div class="ask-question">
            <p>The question</p>
            <div class="ask-person">
                <img src="asker.jpg" />
                <p>Name of Asker</p>
            </div>
        </div>
        <div class="ask-answer">
            <p>Your answer</p>
        </div>
    </div>
    <div class="postmeta">
        <div class="postmeta-time">
            The timestamp
        </div>
        <div class="postmeta-like">
            The number of likes
        </div>
    </div>
</div>
```

You have to style both the question and the credit of the person who sent it in (also known as the *asker*), as well as your answer to the question. Nothing fancy, but it is needed in the markup.

Navigation Links

One last thing within the `div#content`, and that's the navigation between pages. It's helpful to have a "previous" or "next" link when browsing a lot of posts. Those links have to be in the code, and they go just before you close the `div#content` tag. Here's the markup:

```
<div id="navigation">
    <div id="navigation-previous">
        <a href="">Previous</a>
    </div>
    <div id="navigation-next">
        <a href="">Next</a>
    </div>
</div>
```

This puts the Previous link to the left and the Next link to the right.

That does it for the content part of the code, at least for now. Let's take a quick look at the right column, situated in `div#sidebar`.

The Sidebar Column

The right column will consist primarily of the description. It will also need code to show links to any pages that you might have created, have a search box (always a good idea), and some quick links. The user can add just about anything using the description box in the customization screen, since that takes HTML. This is also where you can put nifty things like Twitter boxes and stuff like that, but we'll leave that out for now.

Here's the complete `div#sidebar` code, the HTML markup for the sidebar. This code is really straightforward.

```
<div id="sidebar">
    <div id="sidebar-description">
        Site description goes here
    </div>
    <div id="sidebar-pages">
        <ul>
            <li>If there are pages they'll list here</li>
        </ul>
    </div>
```

```
<div id="sidebar-search">
    <input type="text" value="Search the site" />
    <input type="submit" value="Search &rarr;" />
</div>
<div id="sidebar-quicklinks">
    <ul>
        <li><a href="">RSS link</a></li>
        <li><a href="">Random post</a></li>
        <li><a href="">Browse the archive</a></li>
        <li><a href="">Mobile version</a></li>
    </ul>
</div>
</div>
```

The Footer

Finally, there's the footer at the bottom of the page, which will just contain a link to the top along with some copyright text. Here's the HTML markup:

```
<div id="footer-wrap">
    <div id="footer">
        <div id="footer-left">
            Copyright text
        </div>
        <div id="footer-right">
            <a href="#top"><img src="top.png" /></a>
            <p>Theme credit</p>
        </div>
    </div>
</div>
```

The footer will be in two columns. The left one will contain the copyright notice, and the right one will credit the theme designer (that'd be me in this case!) along with a linked graphic that leads back to the top of the page.

So how does this HTML page look right now? Not good at all, although it would be a bit prettier if we had some dummy images and content in there as Figure 10-5 so clearly shows.

Next, you'll change that by adding some CSS to make the page resemble the mockup!

Want to see how all this code looks together? You can download it from www.wiley.com/go/tacklingtumblr.

NOTE

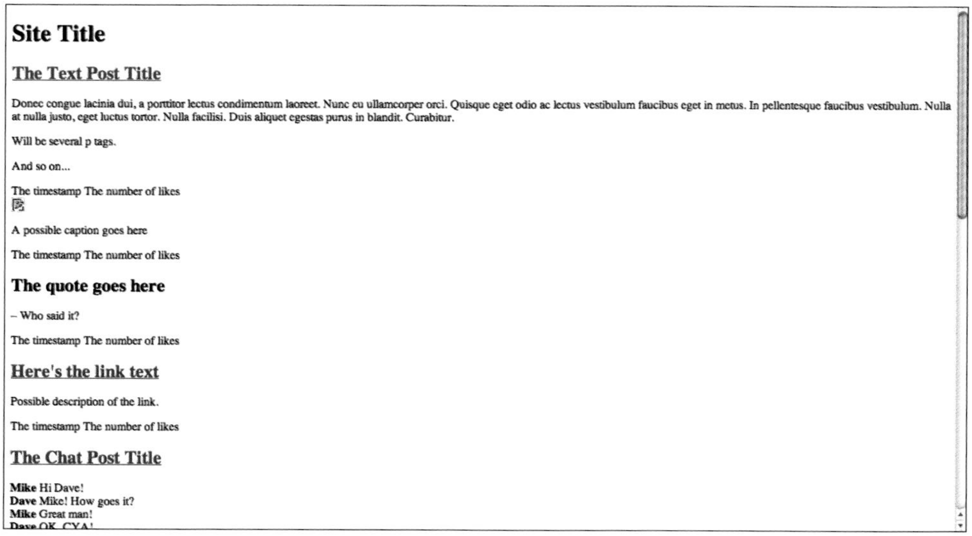

FIGURE 10-5: Unstyled HTML just isn't pretty to look at

Adding the CSS

Now that you have the HTML structure in place you can start styling it. The basic rule is to keep as much design in the CSS as possible. This is especially true for Tumblr themes since you want it to be easy to modify later on, either by just hacking the style part of the theme code or by using the custom CSS feature, which you will enable later in this chapter.

Adding the <style> tag

The CSS goes within style tags in the head section of the theme, as the following code shows:

```
<!DOCTYPE html PUBLIC "-//W3C//DTD XHTML 1.0 Transitional//EN"
  "http://www.w3.org/TR/xhtml1/DTD/xhtml1-transitional.dtd">
<html xmlns="http://www.w3.org/1999/xhtml" xml:lang="en"
  lang="en">
<head>
    <title>Site Title</title>
    <style type="text/css">
        /*CSS goes here */
    </style>
</head>
```

Positioning with CSS

Start by setting some default values for the design, and then position the key div containers such as div#header, div#content, div#sidebar, and div#footer.

```
<style type="text/css">
    body {
        margin: 0;
        padding: 0;
    }
    #site, #header-wrap, #main-wrap, #footer-wrap {
        width: 100%;
        float: left;
    }
    #header, #main, #footer {
        width: 760px;
        margin: 0 auto; /*Centering the div's */
    }
    #content {
        width: 540px;
        float: left;
    }
    #sidebar {
        width: 220px;
        float: right;
    }
    #footer {
        margin-top: 20px;
    }
    #footer-left {
        width: 370px;
        float: left;
    }
    #footer-right {
        width: 370px;
        float: right;
    }
</style>
```

This simple code actually puts everything in its right place and ensures that it will be easy to use elements like div#header-wrap, div#main-wrap, and div#footer-wrap for modifications in the future. Figure 10-6 shows how the HTML renders with this code in.

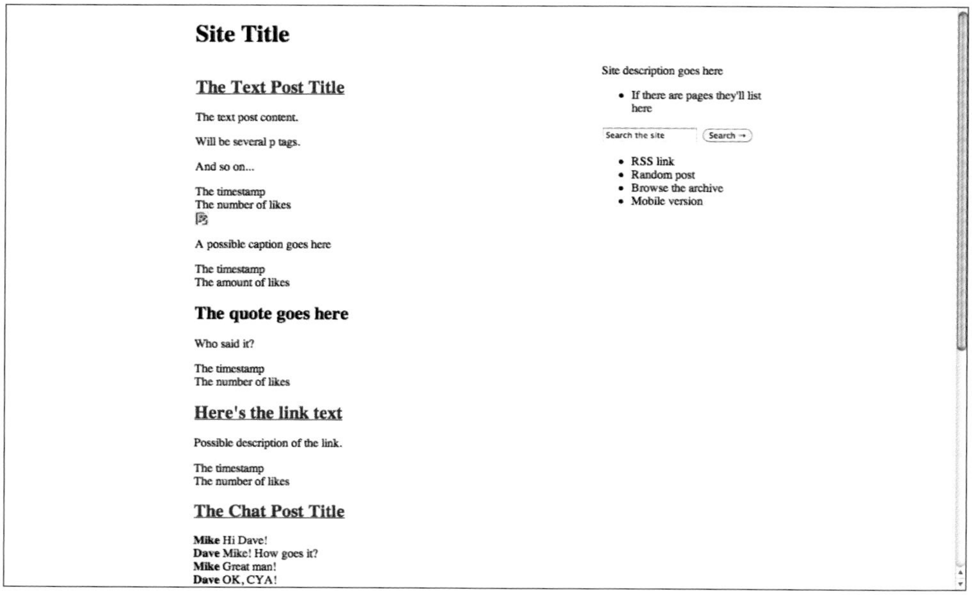

FIGURE 10-6: Some improvement

CSS Reset

Right now just about every tag still has its default value. You don't want that, as tags like `ol` and `ul` work differently depending on where on the site they are used, so add a reset at the top. A *reset* is a bit of CSS meant to remove some default values that are set by browsers.

```
/*RESET */
body, h1, h2, h3, h4, h5, h6,
ol, ul, li, p {
    margin: 0;
    padding: 0;
}
```

Reset code is usually a lot more extensive than that, but I'm keeping it simple here. If you want a good example of a more complete CSS reset, Eric Meyer's is something of a benchmark: `http://meyerweb.com/eric/tools/css/reset/`.

Color and Typography

Let's spice this up with some styles for fonts and colors. While you're at it, make sure to give each part of the CSS its own heading using CSS comments, within the style tag, to make it a bit easier to locate various things in there, and add some basic link styling as well.

```css
/*COLORS AND TYPOGRAPHY */
body {
    background-color: #28446d;
    color: #fff;
}
h1, h2, h3, h4, h5, h6,
#sidebar,
.postmeta {
    font-family: Helvetica, Arial, sans-serif;
}
.site-title {
    font-size: 60px;
    line-height: 60px;
}
h2 {
    font-size: 24px;
    line-height: 24px;
}
.post p {
    font-family: Georgia, "Times New Roman", serif;
}
.text-content p {
    font-size: 16px;
    line-height: 24px;
    margin-bottom: 16px;
}
.postmeta {
    font-size: 12px;
    text-transform: uppercase;
    color: #ddeeff;
}
#sidebar {
    color: #ddeeff;
}
#sidebar ul li, #sidebar ol li {
    list-style: none;
    font-size: 14px;
}
/*LINKS */
h1 a, h2 a {
    color: #fff;
    text-decoration: none;
}
```

```
a:link, a:active, a:visited {
    color: #66bbff;
}
a:hover {
    color: #ffff00;
}
```

Take a look at how the site looks now. Figure 10-7 shows the state of things.

FIGURE 10-7: Now with the right colors

Spacing It

A bit tight, don't you think? Let's add some things to the layout section of the CSS code, to make sure you get that necessary spacing. This is where the post class comes in, since you can use it to make sure the posts don't end up too close to each other. To make it simple to find what you're looking for in the CSS code, I tend to add elements below their top element, which means that the post class, which goes in the div#content container, will be located below #content in the stylesheet.

The following code is the CSS for taking care of the general post things, that is, the post class along with the necessary classes for the postmeta details. That would be the time-stamp and similar parts of the design.

```
.post {
    float: left;
    margin-bottom: 40px;
    padding-right: 20px;
    padding-left: 60px;
}
.postmeta {
    float: left;
    width: 460px;
    margin-top: 20px;
}
.postmeta-time {
    float: left;
    padding-left: 18px;
    padding-right: 15px;
    background: url(icon-postmeta-time.png) left no-repeat;
}
.postmeta-like {
    float: left;
    padding-left: 26px;
    background: url(icon-postmeta-like.png) left no-repeat;
}
```

Notice that postmeta-time and postmeta-like feature background images, small icons to make them a bit more pleasing to the eye, as you might remember from the mockup. These images, along with all other graphics, have to be uploaded to the Tumblr servers when you make an actual theme of this. For now, you can use them locally.

One element that wasn't even in the mockup was the navigation links. This code is the style for those, and should be located at the bottom of post listings:

```
#navigation {
    float: left;
    width: 540px;
    margin-bottom: 20px;
    padding-top: 20px;
    border-top: 1px solid #223344;
    font-size: 18px;
    line-height: 28px;
}
#navigation-previous {
    float: left;
    width: 210px;
```

```
     padding-left: 44px;
     background: url(icon-arrowleft.png) left no-repeat;
}
#navigation-next {
     float: right;
     width: 210px;
     margin-right: 20px;
     padding-right: 44px;
     text-align: right;
     background: url(icon-arrowright.png) right no-repeat;
}
```

Borders and background images make the links look pretty good. Figure 10-8 shows how the bottom of the theme design looks now.

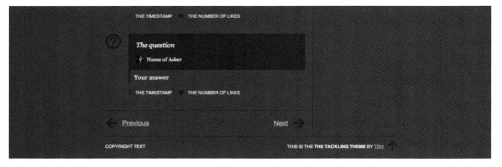

FIGURE 10-8: The footer part of the theme design

Post Type Icons

The theme is starting to look pretty good. Notice that the Ask post is actually designed here, with an icon and some styling. All posts have their icons now, and you can get to them by using the appropriate class. Recall from the earlier HTML section that the post class goes on every post, but we also added dedicated classes for each type of post, including Ask posts. That means that there are classes called text, photo, quote, link, chat, audio, video, and ask being applied to each div container with a post. That means you can easily reach the div you want using CSS, as you can see in the following code.

```
.text {
     background: url(icon-text.png) top left no-repeat;
}
```

```
.photo {
    background: url(icon-photo.png) top left no-repeat;
}
.quote {
    background: url(icon-quote.png) top left no-repeat;
}
.link {
    background: url(icon-link.png) top left no-repeat;
}
.chat {
    background: url(icon-chat.png) top left no-repeat;
}
.audio {
    background: url(icon-audio.png) top left no-repeat;
}
.video {
    background: url(icon-video.png) top left no-repeat;
}
.ask {
    background: url(icon-ask.png) top left no-repeat;
}
```

The actual styling for each type of post, from the background colors of the lines in the chat window to the font choice for quotes in a quote post, is spread across the CSS code. The entire style tag isn't printed here, but you can obviously get it from www.wiley.com/go/tacklingtumblr.

The Final Tweaks to the <style> Tag

First, let's take a look at the finished HTML version. Figure 10-9 shows a text post at the top, and a photo post below it. You get a good view of the sidebar, which has some nice lines separating the various parts of it (not included in the mockup).

Figure 10-10 shows a quote post at the top, followed by a link post, then a chat post with alternating lines, an audio post showing the album art (should that be found), and the top of a video post, which really just looks like a photo post. You already saw the Ask post in Figure 10-8.

FIGURE 10-9: Text and photo posts, along with the header and sidebar

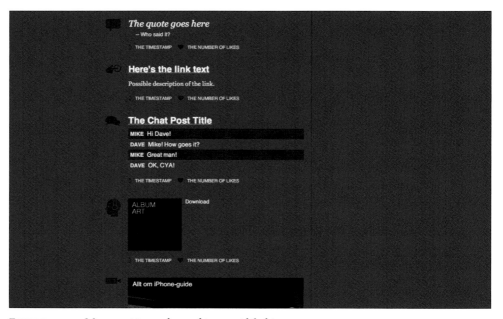

FIGURE 10-10: More post types demoed in a rapid fashion

Most of these posts are pretty easily recreated using CSS on top of the HTML markup. The ones that stand out are the quote post, the chat post, the audio post, and the Ask post. Take a look at the CSS that makes the quote post look the way it does:

```
.quote-content h2 {
    font-family: Georgia, "Times New Roman", serif;
    font-weight: normal;
    font-style: italic;
}
p.quote-source {
    margin-top: 10px;
    padding-left: 20px;
    font-family: Helvetica, Arial, sans-serif;
    font-size: 14px;
    color: #ddeeff;
}
```

The actual quote sits in an h2 heading, and that needs to be styled. You do that by styling all h2 headings within the div.quote-content, and obviously the quote is the only h2 in that div. Next, p.quote-source is the p tag that holds the (optional) quote source, and you've got some styling there, too. Pretty straightforward.

Here's the CSS for the chat post:

```
.chat-content {
    margin-top: 10px;
}
.chat-lines strong {
    padding-right: 5px;
    color: #ddeeff;
    font-size: 14px;
    text-transform: uppercase;
}
.line {
    padding: 5px;
}
.odd {
    background-color: #223344;
}
```

The interesting part here is the styling for all the strong tags within the `div.chat-lines` tag. Recall that `strong` is used to highlight the person talking, so you want it to look a bit different.

Each thing that's being said in the chat transcript sits in a div with the `line` class, which has padding to make it look better with the background that every other line has. From Tumblr you get the classes `odd` for odd numbered lines, and `even` for lines that are even numbers. Adding a background color to the `odd` class, gives you a background on every other line, making the transcript easier to read.

Let's move on to the audio post:

```
.audio-content {
    width: 100%;
    float: left;
}
.audio-album {
    float: left;
    width: 150px;
}
.audio-player {
    float: left;
    margin-bottom: 10px;
}
.audio-player-meta {
    font-size: 14px;
}
```

The thing that sets the audio post apart is that it might feature album art, and you need to make sure that ends up in a nice place. It also has to work well with the actual audio player (not present in the HTML file) and the download link. Put all this within the `div.audio-content`, and then put the album art and the player in individual divss. This way you can make sure that everything aligns properly; the album art will float left thanks to the `audio-album` class, and in the same fashion, the player along with the download link will end up beside the album art. By letting the download link and the player share the same div you can easily control how they line up to the album art. Take a look at the HTML code again to get a better overview of how the tags relate to one another.

Finally, take a look at the necessary CSS for the Ask code:

```css
.ask-question {
    padding: 20px;
    background-color: #223344;
}
.ask-question p {
    font-size: 18px;
    font-style: italic;
}
.ask-person {
    margin-top: 20px;
}
.ask-person img {
    float: left;
    margin-right: 10px;
}
.ask-person p {
    font-size: 14px;
    line-height: 18px;
    font-style: normal;
}
.ask-answer {
    padding-top: 1px;
    padding-bottom: 5px;
    padding-left: 10px;
    border-left: 5px solid #223344;
}
.ask-answer p {
    margin-top: 10px;
    margin-bottom: 0;
}
```

This section really isn't all that tricky, but it does feature floating of the asking person's Tumblr avatar (see `.ask-person img` in the code) and some use of background colors and borders. I just wanted to show that you can do a lot with padding in the right place.

That concludes the CSS part of the theme. No doubt you'll have some things to tweak when you get ready to release the theme, and it might still not validate, but for now this will do. Next you'll add Tumblr tags to the HTML and CSS.

Want to see where we stand now, or just check out the full CSS? You can download it from www.wiley.com/go/tacklingtumblr. **NOTE**

Adding Tumblr Tags

Now that you've got both HTML and CSS ready it is time to start creating the actual Tumblr theme. For this example, create a brand new file called `tackling.html` and use that file to populate the code with the Tumblr tags. When the most obvious tags are in, you will preview the theme on Tumblr.

The Head Section

First fill the head section with the necessary tags. The head is pretty sparse right now, containing a title and the style tag only. Add the following code:

```
<meta name="color:Background" content="#28446d" />
<meta http-equiv="Content-Type" content="text/html;
  charset=utf-8" />
<title>{block:PostSummary}{PostSummary} -
  {/block:PostSummary}{Title}</title>
<meta name="title" content="{block:PostSummary}{PostSummary} -
  {/block:PostSummary}{Title}" />
<meta name="description" content="{block:PostSummary}
  {PostSummary} - {/block:PostSummary}{Title} - {Description}"
<meta name="keywords" content="{block:Permalink}{block:Posts}
  {block:Tags}{Tag}, {/block:Tags}{/block:Posts}
  {/block:Permalink}" />
<link rel="shortcut icon" href="{Favicon}" />
<link rel="apple-touch-icon" href="{PortraitURL-128}"/>
<link rel="alternate" type="application/rss+xml" href="{RSS}" />
```

The first line is for letting users pick their own background color, with the color previously stated in the style block (now removed) set as default. Line two is the content type for the browser. After that is the SEO discussed in Chapter 9, with a proper title tag and meta blocks for title, description, and keywords. Use the {Favicon} tag to get an icon based on the user avatar. That same avatar is used for bookmarking on Apple's iOS devices (and more). The RSS declaration wraps up the code.

> **NOTE** Remember that everything between curly brackets are Tumblr tags, so {RSS} and {Favicon} are both Tumblr tags. If tags say `block` at the beginning they need to be closed as well; for example, {block:Tags} is the opening tag and {/block:Tags} is the closing tag. See Chapter 9 for more information on Tumblr tags.

Next comes the style tag with your CSS tags. The only thing you do here is swap out the body color for `{color:Background}`, which comes from the `meta` tag in the head section. This lets the user change the background color. The code is really simple:

```
body {
    background: {color:Background};
}
```

Your next edit will be the site title, which resides in `div#header`:

```
<div id="header-wrap">
    <div id="header">
        <h1 class="site-title">
            <a href="/" name="top">Site Title</a>
        </h1>
    </div>
</div>
```

Swap out `Site Title` within the link that sits in `h1.site-title`, for `{Title}` and you're all set, like this:

```
<div id="header-wrap">
    <div id="header">
        <h1 class="site-title">
            <a href="/" name="top">{Title}</a>
        </h1>
    </div>
</div>
```

Now the site title will be the actual site title, instead of something hard coded in the theme.

The Content

The actual content is the tricky part. Here you'll have a lot of block tags so that Tumblr knows what to load. Basically, you wrap each part of your HTML code into the corresponding block tag. So the first post in the HTML code, the text post, goes in the corresponding Tumblr tag block, which is `{block:Text}`, like this:

```
{block:Text}
    <!-- Text Post -->
    <div class="post text">
        <h2>
```

```
            <a href="">The Text Post Title</a>
        </h2>
        <div class="text-content">
            <p>Donec congue lacinia dui, a porttitor lectus
              condimentum laoreet. Nunc eu ullamcorper orci.
              Quisque eget odio ac lectus vestibulum faucibus
              eget in metus. In pellentesque faucibus
              vestibulum. Nulla at nulla justo, eget luctus
              tortor. Nulla facilisi. Duis aliquet egestas purus
              in blandit. Curabitur.</p>
            <p>Will be several p tags.</p>
            <p>And so on...</p>
        </div>
        <div class="postmeta">
            <span class="postmeta-time">
                The timestamp
            </span>
            <span class="postmeta-like">
                The number of likes
            </span>
        </div>
    </div>
{/block:Text}
```

This code tells Tumblr to use the content in between the {block:Text} tags when a text post is supposed to be output. The same is true for photo posts, with {block:Photo} instead of {block:Text} and so on. All these blocks will go inside the {block:Post} tag, which tells Tumblr that this is the part where all the post content is. {block:Post} looks something like this:

```
{block:Posts}

    <!-- Text Post -->
    {block:Text}
    <div class="post text">
        <!-- Output code -->
    </div>
    {/block:Text}

    <!-- Photo Post -->
    {block:Photo}
    <div class="post photo">
```

```
    <!-- Output code -->
</div>
{/block:Photo}

<!-- Quote Post -->
{block:Quote}
<div class="post quote">
    <!-- Output code -->
</div>
{/block:Quote}

<!-- Link Post -->
{block:Link}
<div class="post link">
    <!-- Output content -->
</div>
{/block:Link}

<!-- Chat Post -->
{block:Chat}
<div class="post chat">
    <!-- Output content -->
</div>
{/block:Chat}

<!-- Audio Post -->
{block:Audio}
<div class="post audio">
    <!-- Output content -->
</div>
{/block:Audio}

<!-- Video Post -->
{block:Video}
<div class="post video">
    <!-- Output content -->
</div>
{/block:Video}

<!-- Ask -->
{block:Answer}
<div class="post ask">
    <!-- Output content -->
```

```
    </div>
    {/block:Answer}

{/block:Posts}
```

Let's start with the text post. A title is optional so wrap it in {block:Title}, and then change the title from the dummy "The Text Post Title" to {Title}, which outputs the post title. The link should point to {Permalink}, which leads to the post. The content, which is a bunch of p tags filled with nonsense right now, has to be swapped for {Body}.

Finally there's the postmeta, which you'll reuse for all posts although it's only covered here. The timestamp belongs in a block called {block:Date}, and you can output how long ago the post was published with {TimeAgo}. The like count sits in a block called {block:NoteCount}, and the actual count is outputted with {NoteCount}.

Here's the final code for the text posts:

```
<!-- Text Post -->
{block:Text}
<div class="post text">
    {block:Title}
    <h2>
        <a href="{Permalink}">{Title}</a>
    </h2>
    {/block:Title}
    <div class="text-content">
        {Body}
    </div>
    <div class="postmeta">
        {block:Date}
        <span class="postmeta-time">
            <a href="{Permalink}">{TimeAgo}</a>
        </span>
        {/block:Date}
        {block:NoteCount}
        <span class="postmeta-like">
            {NoteCount}
        </span>
        {/block:NoteCount}
    </div>
</div>
{/block:Text}
```

Photo posts sit in {block:Photo} blocks and you use the same postmeta as for text posts. Around the image are {LinkOpenTag} and {LinkCloseTag}, which make the image a clickable link if one is set in the post. {PhotoURL-500} adds an src to the img tag. The number is the pixel width of the photo, and there are a number of options available. The {PhotoAlt} provides the image with an alt text.

Finally, the {block:Caption} block is only used if there's a caption set for the image, and {Caption} obviously outputs it. Here's the code:

```
<!-- Photo Post -->
{block:Photo}
<div class="post photo">
    <div class="photo-content">
        <div class="photo-img">
            {LinkOpenTag}
                <img src="{PhotoURL-500}" alt="{PhotoAlt}" />
            {LinkCloseTag}
        </div>
        {block:Caption}
            {Caption}
        {/block:Caption}
    </div>
    <div class="postmeta">
        {block:Date}
        <span class="postmeta-time">
            <a href="{Permalink}">{TimeAgo}</a>
        </span>
        {/block:Date}
        {block:NoteCount}
        <span class="postmeta-like">
            {NoteCount}
        </span>
        {/block:NoteCount}
    </div>
</div>
{/block:Photo}
```

Quote posts go inside the {block:Quote} tag. The actual quote is just a {Quote} tag, but the source of the quote is optional so it needs to be inside the {block:Source} tag, with {Source} outputting its content. I'm sure you've figured out how it works by now: Block tags almost always contain a similar tag without the block part to output the actual content. Here's the code for the quote posts:

```
<!-- Quote Post -->
{block:Quote}
<div class="post quote">
    <div class="quote-content">
        <h2>{Quote}</h2>
        {block:Source}
        <p class="quote-source">&ndash; {Source}</p>
        {/block:Source}
    </div>
    <div class="postmeta">
        {block:Date}
        <span class="postmeta-time">
            <a href="{Permalink}">{TimeAgo}</a>
        </span>
        {/block:Date}
        {block:NoteCount}
        <span class="postmeta-like">
            {NoteCount}
        </span>
        {/block:NoteCount}
    </div>
</div>
{/block:Quote}
```

Link posts are pretty simple. The URL of the link is just {URL}, but because some people prefer to set a target for the link, such as "open in a new browser," you also need to add {Target} to your link tag (the a tag, that is). The chosen linked text is just {Name}, and should there be a description, you use {block:Description}, and {Description} inside of it.

Here's the code:

```
<!-- Link Post -->
{block:Link}
<div class="post link">
    <div class="link-content">
        <h2>
            <a href="{URL}" {Target}>{Name}</a>
        </h2>
        {block:Description}
            {Description}
        {/block:Description}
```

```
        </div>
        <div class="postmeta">
            {block:Date}
            <span class="postmeta-time">
                <a href="{Permalink}"><a href="{Permalink}">
                {TimeAgo}</a></a>
            </span>
            {/block:Date}
            {block:NoteCount}
            <span class="postmeta-like">
                {NoteCount}
            </span>
            {/block:NoteCount}
        </div>
    </div>
{/block:Link}
```

Chat post follows the same structure, except for the {block:Lines}, which outputs the actual lines. If you want some control over how the lines look, like swapping colors, you need to add {Alt} to the class of the line. It's good practice to add user_{UserNumber} to the class, which will output a unique class called user_X where X is a number to identify the user in the transcript. Also, {block:Label} goes around the name, and {Label} outputs it. {Line} outputs the actual transcript line, excluding the label obviously.

Here's the code:

```
<!-- Chat Post -->
{block:Chat}
<div class="post chat">
    {block:Title}
    <h2>
        <a href="{Permalink}">{Title}</a>
    </h2>
    {/block:Title}
    <div class="chat-content">
        <div class="chat-lines">
            {block:Lines}
            <div class="line {Alt} user_{UserNumber}">
                {block:Label}
                    <strong>{Label}</strong>
                {/block:Label}
                {Line}
```

```
            </div>
            {/block:Lines}
        </div>
    </div>
    <div class="postmeta">
        {block:Date}
        <span class="postmeta-time">
            <a href="{Permalink}">{TimeAgo}</a>
        </span>
        {/block:Date}
        {block:NoteCount}
        <span class="postmeta-like">
            {NoteCount}
        </span>
        {/block:NoteCount}
    </div>
</div>
{/block:Chat}
```

For audio posts, use `{block:AlbumArt}` to show album art if there is any. The image source is returned by `{AlbumArtURL}`, and if the track's name is provided, you output that as alt text using `{block:TrackName}` and `{TrackName}`. The actual player is returned using `{AudioPlayerWhite}` (yes, there are color variants) and you can also add captions using the now familiar `{block:Caption}` and `{Caption}`. Finally, `{block:External Audio}` lets you output a download link, with `{ExternalAutioURL}` as the URL to the actual file.

This is the first appearance of a localized string. `{lang:Download}` will automatically translate `Download` to its equivalent in any language that Tumblr supports. There aren't too many strings you can use this way, but the ones that exist — like `Download` — can be prefixed with `lang` to get the translation.

Here's the audio post code:

```
<!-- Audio Post -->
{block:Audio}
<div class="post audio">
    <div class="audio-content">
        {block:AlbumArt}
        <div class="audio-album">
            <img src="{AlbumArtURL}"
              alt="{block:TrackName}{TrackName}
```

```
                {/block:TrackName}" />
        </div>
        {/block:AlbumArt}
        <div class="audio-player">
            {AudioPlayerWhite}
        </div>
        <div class="audio-player-meta">
            {block:Caption}
            <div class="audio-caption">
                {Caption}
            </div>
            {/block:Caption}
            {block:ExternalAudio}
                <a href="{ExternalAudioURL}">
                    {lang:Download}</a></span>
            {/block:ExternalAudio}
        </div>
    </div>
    <div class="postmeta">
        {block:Date}
        <span class="postmeta-time">
            <a href="{Permalink}">{TimeAgo}</a>
        </span>
        {/block:Date}
        {block:NoteCount}
        <span class="postmeta-like">
            {NoteCount}
        </span>
        {/block:NoteCount}
    </div>
</div>
{/block:Audio}
```

The video post type is almost identical to the photo one, but with fewer tags and using tags named video instead. Here's the code:

```
<!-- Video Post -->
{block:Video}
<div class="post video">
    <div class="video-content">
        <div class="video-player">
            {Video-500}
```

```
        </div>
        {block:Caption}
            {Caption}
        {/block:Caption}
    </div>
    <div class="postmeta">
        {block:Date}
        <span class="postmeta-time">
            <a href="{Permalink}">{TimeAgo}</a>
        </span>
        {/block:Date}
        {block:NoteCount}
        <span class="postmeta-like">
            {NoteCount}
        </span>
        {/block:NoteCount}
    </div>
</div>
{/block:Video}
```

The Ask posts belong in `{block:Answer}` tags, and the question gets outputted by `{Question}`. You get the name of the one who's asking with `{Asker}`, and you can get his user's avatar with `{AskerPortraitURL-24}`, where the number, which stands for the size in pixels of the user avatar, is interchangeable just as with other tags you've seen. Finally, output the answer with `{Answer}` and you get this code:

```
<!-- Ask -->
{block:Answer}
<div class="post ask">
    <div class="ask-content">
        <div class="ask-question">
            {Question}
            <div class="ask-person">
                <img src="{AskerPortraitURL-24}" />
                <p>{Answer}</p>
            </div>
        </div>
        <div class="ask-answer">
            {Answer}
        </div>
    </div>
    <div class="postmeta">
```

```
        {block:Date}
        <span class="postmeta-time">
            <a href="{Permalink}">{TimeAgo}</a>
        </span>
        {/block:Date}
        {block:NoteCount}
        <span class="postmeta-like">
            {NoteCount}
        </span>
        {/block:NoteCount}
    </div>
</div>
{/block:Answer}
```

Navigation Links

Before you close {block:Posts} with {/block:Posts}, you need to add the navigation links so that people can jump between pages. This code is not particularly complicated. It all sits in {block:Navigation}, and includes two separate blocks for the previous and next pages. Here's the code:

```
<!-- Navigation -->
{block:Pagination}
<div id="navigation">
    {block:PreviousPage}
    <div id="navigation-previous">
        <a href="{PreviousPage}">{lang:Previous}</a>
    </div>
    {/block:PreviousPage}
    {block:NextPage}
    <div id="navigation-next">
        <a href="{NextPage}">{lang:Next page}</a>
    </div>
    {/block:NextPage}
</div>
{/block:Pagination}
```

Sidebar

That's it for the posts part, for now. Next you'll add the necessities to the sidebar and then give this theme a go in the Tumblr customization area.

Every Tumblr theme needs a description, and you add that with {block:Description}, with {Description} within.

{block:HasPages} shows up only if there are pages such as About or contact pages to show. Inside {block:HasPages}, another block, {block:Pages}, uses the now familiar {URL} and {Label} to output the actual pages.

The search form is simple, with one input field for the search query (with {SearchQuery} as a data carrier), and one for submitting the search. Notice the use of {lang:Search} to make sure that the text on the search button is localized when possible.

Finally, you wrap this up with links to the RSS feed, the archive, the mobile site, and the ever-interesting random post feature. These are all basic features, and all but the RSS feed point to hard-coded URLs that will take care of the rest. The actual link text is localized as you can see.

Here is the full div#sidebar code:

```html
<!-- SIDE COLUMN -->
<div id="sidebar">
    {block:Description}
    <div id="sidebar-description">
        {Description}
    </div>
    {/block:Description}

    {block:HasPages}
    <div id="sidebar-pages">
        <ul>
            {block:Pages}
            <li>
                <a href="{URL}">{Label}</a>
            </li>
            {/block:Pages}
        </ul>
    </div>
    {/block:HasPages}

    <div id="sidebar-search">
        <form action="/search" method="get">
            <input type="text" name="q" value="{SearchQuery}"/>
            <input type="submit" value="{lang:Search}"/>
        </form>
    </div>
</div>
```

```
<div id="sidebar-quicklinks">
    <ul>
        <li><a href="{RSS}">{lang:RSS feed}</a></li>
        <li><a href="/random">{lang:Random}</a></li>
        <li><a href="/archive">{lang:Archive}</a></li>
        <li><a href="/mobile">{lang:Mobile}</a></li>
    </ul>
</div>
</div>
```

Checking the Results

It's about time to take a look at how this looks on Tumblr now, don't you think? Figure 10-11 shows how the theme renders when you paste the code into the Custom HTML box under Theme on the customization screen.

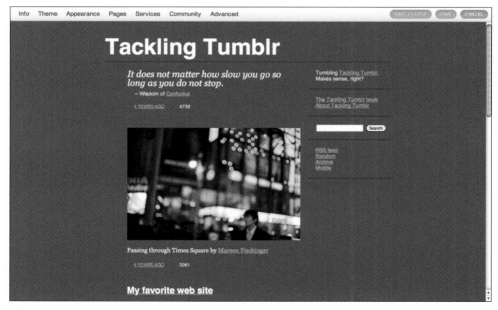

FIGURE 10-11: Hey, look, you've got a theme!

Remember the `{color:Background}` tag? As Figure 10-12 shows, you can pick your very own background color under Appearance, and reset the default as well.

FIGURE 10-12: Not my favorite color, but I did pick it myself

There is a problem here, however, and that is the lack of images. This theme is pretty boring without the icons, right? Upload them from `http://www.tumblr.com/themes/upload_static_file`, where you can browse your computer and upload one file at a time, as you can see in Figure 10-13. This is a bit tedious: there are nine icons, two postmeta icons, the background, and three arrows, so you need to upload a total of 14 files.

FIGURE 10-13: Uploading file by file

As Figure 10-13 also shows, you get the URL to the file after each upload, along with the option to upload again.

| NOTE | Your uploaded file URLs aren't remembered anywhere, so copy them to a safe place right away. You can't edit uploaded files either. |

Are you done with the theme? Not quite, but before you dive into Disqus support and show-ing notes and reblogs, take a look at the theme in action on the Tackling Tumblr website, as shown in Figure 10-14.

FIGURE 10-14: The theme is live on http://tackling.tumblr.com

Want to download the theme as it is at this stage? Then grab version 0.3 of the Tackling theme from www.wiley.com/go/tacklingtumblr. **NOTE**

Adding More Features

There are a ton of things you can add to your Tackling Tumblr theme (or any theme). Besides the obvious such as Twitter widgets, Facebook fan boxes, and last plays from Last.fm, there are some others that are highly recommended.

Adding Notes

One feature you may want to add is notes. A *note* is the box at the bottom of a post that shows all the actions other users have taken with the post, such as likes and reblogs. Figure

10-15 shows the notes block from a post on the Tumblr staff blog (`http://staff`
`.tumblr.com`) about pledges to Japan after the March 2011 tsunami.

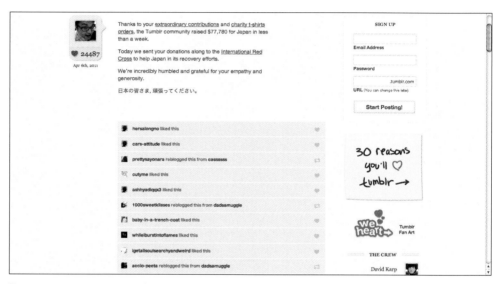

FIGURE 10-15: Notes example from http://staff.tumblr.com/post/4395299066/japan-donations-recap

Adding notes to your single post view (because you obviously don't want a mammoth list of
1000+ likes and reblogs on your front page) is easy. All you have to do is add `{PostNotes}`
before the closing `{/block:Post}` tag. In the Tackling theme, that means adding it just
after the Ask block, and before `{/block:Post}`, as highlighted in the following code:

```
<!-- Ask -->
{block:Answer}
<div class="post ask">
    <div class="ask-content">
        <div class="ask-question">
            {Question}
            <div class="ask-person">
                <img src="{AskerPortraitURL-24}" />
                <p>{Answer}</p>
            </div>
        </div>
        <div class="ask-answer">
            {Answer}
        </div>
```

```
        </div>
        <div class="postmeta">
            {block:Date}
            <span class="postmeta-time">
                <a href="{Permalink}">{TimeAgo}</a>
            </span>
            {/block:Date}
            {block:NoteCount}
            <span class="postmeta-like">
                {NoteCount}
            </span>
            {/block:NoteCount}
        </div>
    </div>
    {/block:Answer}

    {PostNotes}
{/block:Posts}
```

{PostNotes} displays only on single post pages, or permalink pages as they are often called, so you needn't worry about its existence in listings. If you need more control around your notes, you can use {block:PostNotes}, which also displays only on permalink pages, but can contain more information such as headers or other elements you might like to display on permalink pages only.

Recall this code block from every postmeta in the Tackling theme:

```
{block:NoteCount}
<span class="postmeta-like">
    {NoteCount}
</span>
{/block:NoteCount}
```

{block:NoteCount} shows only if the post has any notes, and {NoteCount} shows the number of notes. You could also use {NoteCountWithLabel}, which will output something like "53 notes" instead of {NoteCount}, but still wrap it within the {block:NoteCount} block.

Adding the {PostNotes} tag makes the notes appear on a single post page, but they won't look good unless you do a little more work. Take a look at Figure 10-16; that's not a pretty list at all, is it?

FIGURE 10-16: An unattractive list of likes and reblogs

Luckily this problem is easily remedied. {PostNotes} results in an `ol` tag with a `li` for each like or reblog in the list. It goes something like this:

```
<ol class="notes">
    <li class="note like without_commentary tumblog_X">
        <!-- This is a like without commentary -->
    </li>
    <li class="note reblog without_commentary tumblog_X">
        <!-- This is a reblog without commentary -->
    </li>
    <li class="note like with_commentarytumblog_X">
        <!-- This is a like with commentary -->
    </li>
    <li class="note reblog with_commentary tumblog_X">
        <!-- This is a reblog with commentary -->
    </li>
</ol>
```

Notice that the wrapping `ol` has the class `notes`, and every `li` has the class `note`. After that, the markup depends on what kind of note it is. Every `li` that is a like gets the class `like`, and reblogs get the class `reblog`. However, when reblogging you can add your comments, so there are `with_commentary` and `without_commentary` classes as well. Finally, every `li` also gets a class showing what Tumblr site it is from, so `tumblog_X` in the preceding code really stands for `tumblog_SITENAME`, or `tumblog_tackling` for example. That way you can make select sites look different.

Now you have all you need to make this thing pretty! The next step is to style `ol.notes`, and `li.note` for some general style for every list item. You could also pinpoint what's a reblog and what's a like. Finally, it might be a good idea to do something about the notes with commentary; they looked really bad in Figure 10-16, didn't they?

Here is the CSS added to the style tag in the Tackling theme's head section:

```css
ol.notes {
    float: left;
    width: 480px;
    margin-left: 60px;
    margin-bottom: 20px;
    padding-top: 5px;
    border-top: 1px solid #223344;
}
li.note {
    font-family: Helvetica, Arial, sans-serif;
    font-size: 12px;
    line-height: 16px;
    text-transform: uppercase;
    color: #223344;
    padding: 5px 0;
    border-bottom: 1px solid #223344;
    list-style: none;
}
li.note img {
    float: left;
    margin-right: 10px;
}
li.note blockquote {
    margin: 5px 5px 0 0;
    padding: 10px;
    background: #375470;
    text-transform: none;
}
li.note blockquote a {
    text-decoration: none;
    color: #fff;
}
```

Nothing too fancy here. The `img` tag is used for the user avatar, which is floating to the left. Likewise, the `blockquote` tag is where any commentary from the noting user sits, so that needed some styling, along with its content which is all a link.

Figure 10-17 shows the end result.

FIGURE 10-17: Now the notes look a bit better

That's it for the notes; now for something a bit more complicated.

Adding Disqus Support

As you know by now, Tumblr doesn't have its own commenting solution, and the most commonly used tool is Disqus. Chapter 7 covers working with comments in detail, but if you're creating a theme you might want to use that fancy sitename solution that lets the user just input the Disqus sitename in the theme settings to get comments up and running.

For this example you will use the custom text feature, which lets you collect custom text strings from the theme settings. It is much like the `color:Background` name that you used with the `meta` tag in head previously. Call this one `text:Disqus shortname`, and where `color:Background` had a default color as the content, `text:Disqus shortname` will be empty by default because you don't want it to actually preload a specific Disqus site.

Add the following line just below the `meta` tag with `color:Background`, within the head section:

```
<meta name="text:Disqus Shortname" content="" />
```

This code enables a pretty little box where the user can input the Disqus sitename (covered in Chapter 7). The result is shown in Figure 10-18.

FIGURE 10-18: The Tackling theme now has a box for your Disqus sitename

That's the first of three major steps to get Disqus to work properly with the theme. The second is to add the actual code that outputs Disqus. You could grab this from `http://disqus.com/admin/tumblr/`, but then it will be site specific. You want it to use the data from that little Disqus input box in the theme settings, right?

The solution is to use `{text:Disqus Shortname}`, which is the Tumblr tag you enabled using the `meta` tag previously. Everywhere in the Disqus code where the sitename is hard coded, put `{text:Disqus Shortname}` instead. Then wrap the Disqus code within a `{block:IfDisqusShortname}` block that shows only if a Disqus sitename is supplied. Inside of `{block:IfDisqusShortname}`, wrap the rest within a `{block:PermalinkPage}` block to make sure that the code will load only on single posts, since you won't need it on the front page, for example.

Following is the end result, and should be placed after you have closed the `{/block:Posts}` tag:

```
{block:IfDisqusShortname}
    {block:PermalinkPage}

        <script type="text/javascript">var disqus_url =
          "{Permalink}"; var disqus_title
          ="{block:PostTitle}{PostTitle}{/block:PostTitle}";
          </script>{block:Permalink}<div id="disqus_thread">
          </div>
        <script type="text/javascript">
          /**
            *var disqus_identifier; [Optional but recommended:
              Define a unique identifier (e.g. post id or slug)
```

```
        for this thread]
      */
    (function() {
     var dsq = document.createElement('script'); dsq.type
       = 'text/javascript'; dsq.async = true;
     dsq.src = 'http://{text:Disqus Shortname}.disqus.com
       /embed.js';
     (document.getElementsByTagName('head')[0] ||
       document.getElementsByTagName('body')[0])
       .appendChild(dsq);
     })();
    </script>
    <noscript>Please enable JavaScript to view the <a
      href="http://disqus.com/?ref_noscript={text:Disqus
      Shortname}">comments powered by Disqus.</a></noscript>
    {/block:Permalink}<script type="text/javascript">
    var disqus_shortname = '{text:Disqus Shortname}';
    (function () {
      var s = document.createElement('script'); s.async =
        true;
      s.src = 'http://{text:Disqus Shortname}.disqus.com
        /count.js';
      (document.getElementsByTagName('HEAD')[0] ||
        document.getElementsByTagName('BODY')[0])
        .appendChild(s);
    }());
    </script>

  {/block:PermalinkPage}
{/block:IfDisqusShortname}
```

Now you have Disqus commenting capabilities on your site, assuming you've filled out the Disqus shortname, as Figure 10-18 showed. However, without styling, the Disqus comments won't look good in the Tackling theme (see Figure 10-19), so you need to make sure everything aligns properly.

You don't want to add too much styling to Disqus because the CSS can be modified from the Disqus side of things. You just want to make sure the comments and the comment box align properly with your content, which is not the case right now.

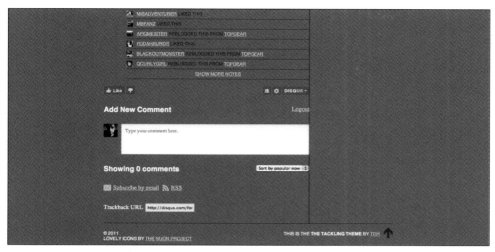

FIGURE 10-19: Disqus is loading on permalink pages, but it is not pretty

The solution for this is `div#disqus_thread`, the wrapping div that contains both the comments and the box for leaving comments. Here's the simple code for that:

```
div#disqus_thread {
    margin-bottom: 20px;
    padding-left: 60px;
    padding-right: 20px;
}
```

Anything more fancy than that will have to be done from within the Disqus interface, which makes sense because Disqus has features for it as well as various themes and services you might want to use.

The end result isn't all that different from the previous one, but it does align better with the rest of the site, as you can see in Figure 10-20.

FIGURE 10-20: Now the Disqus comments align appropriately

You're almost done with the Disqus comments; there's only one more thing to add. If you have Disqus comments enabled, wouldn't you want to show the comment count on the front page as well?

The solution is simple. Just add the following code to the postmeta section:

```
{block:IfDisqusShortname}
<span class="postmeta-disqus">
    <a class="dsq-comment-count"
       href="{Permalink}#disqus_thread">Comments</a>
</span>
{/block:IfDisqusShortname}
```

In the case of the Tackling theme, that is a bit of a nuisance because you repeat the post-meta section for every post at this time. That's to make it easy to remove the postmeta from some types of post, but not from all of them, as you'll remember. You want Disqus comments to go in all the postmeta sections, so you have to add them.

This means the entire postmeta section now looks like the following for every post type:

```
<div class="postmeta">
    {block:Date}
    <span class="postmeta-time">
        <a href="{Permalink}">{TimeAgo}</a>
```

```
    </span>
    {/block:Date}
    {block:NoteCount}
    <span class="postmeta-like">
        {NoteCount}
    </span>
    {/block:NoteCount}
    like
    <span class="postmeta-disqus">
        <a class="dsq-comment-count"
          href="{Permalink}#disqus_thread">Comments</a>
    </span>
    {/block:IfDisqusShortname}
</div>
```

The principle for showing the comment count in the postmeta div is the same as for the Disqus box; {block:IfDisqusShortname} will show its contents only if there's a Disqus sitename applied. Within the {block:IfDisqusShortname}, the markup and style is in the same lines as for the other postmeta elements, meaning that you'll have to find a nice little icon for span.postmeta-disqus to make sure it looks just as nice as span.postmeta-time and span.postmeta-like. I have added an icon image to the postmeta part of the CSS in the style tag:

```
.postmeta-disqus {
    float: left;
    padding-left: 26px;
    background: url(http://static.tumblr.com/qjswrnx/
      An11kl91t/icon-postmeta-disqus.png) left no-repeat;
}
```

The end result? Well, thanks to the Disqus code snippet and the styling for the postmeta element, along with span.postmeta-disqus which makes sure the icon ends up where it should, you can now see how many comments each post has to the right of the number of notes below each post. Figure 10-21 shows a post that was published two hours ago, with 0 comments.

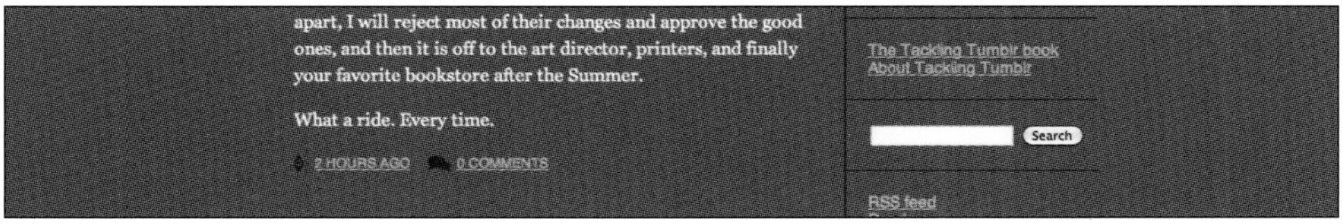

FIGURE 10-21: Comment count added to the postmeta section

That's it; the Tackling theme is now Disqus-ready, without the need to hack any theme code for the end user.

Adding Custom CSS Capability

One last little thing before we close the book on the Tackling theme for now. Chances are there are some things the user might want to alter here, things that really just are a few lines of CSS. So why not add a box for some custom CSS? There is a great little tag for that, {CustomCSS}, which usually sits within its own `style` tag after the one you actually use. This tag will let the user add additional CSS rules or overwrite original ones, which can come in handy.

Add this line directly after the closing `style` tag in head:

```
<style type="text/css">{CustomCSS}</style>
```

Now you offer the option to add some custom CSS, which loads after the full `style` tag with the actual theme CSS, using the *Add custom CSS* box (under Advanced on the customization screen). Figure 10-22 shows the result, and that wraps up your work with the Tackling theme for now.

FIGURE 10-22: Add some custom CSS to the Tackling theme

Want to download the Tackling theme as it is at this stage? You can get it from `www.wiley.com/go/tacklingtumblr` for free.

NOTE

Keep up with the Tackling theme and all its updates at `http://tackling.tumblr.com`.

Submitting Your Theme to the Theme Garden

Anyone can submit a theme to the Tumblr Theme Garden. Keep in mind that if you submit a theme and it is approved, your theme will become available for anyone to use.

There are some rules for the themes you submit:

- The theme must support all types of posts (text, photo, quote, link, chat, audio, and video).

- All external assets you need, such as images and JavaScript libraries, must be hosted with Tumblr. You'll have to use the static file uploader when submitting assets to Tumblr: `http://www.tumblr.com/themes/upload_static_file`.

- The theme must be less than 64 KB in size. Most themes fit everything in a single file (the code that goes in the Source code box when you submit your theme), but you could put CSS and JavaScript code in external files and use the static file uploader.

- Standard Tumblr tags must be used when appropriate. Use {RSS} for linking the RSS feed, use {MetaDescription}, {Favicon}, and so on. Don't hardcode stuff in HTML if there is a Tumblr tag you can use.

- Third-party content must be optional. You can't force in Disqus code or a Twitter widget; instead use custom text to make these things work if you want to support them out of the box.

- The theme must look really good. Tumblr doesn't want themes in the Theme Garden that don't meet its aesthetic requirements, so if your theme doesn't look as if it would fit in you'll have to make do with the Custom HTML feature, or host it elsewhere. Of course, you can design your own site any way you want; this is just for submitting a theme to the Theme Garden!

Tumblr's theme moderators will review your submitted theme, and if they approve, it will be posted on the Theme Garden. If not, well, too bad, you'll have to edit the theme and try again if you want it made available for download from the Theme Garden.

Submitting the theme is easy. Make sure you're logged in to Tumblr and go to the theme submit page (`http://www.tumblr.com/themes/new`), shown in Figure 10-23, and fill out the form. The Title field is for your theme name and the Source code box is for the actual theme code. You'll also be asked to upload a screenshot of the theme in either JPG or PNG format, with the size of 375×250 pixels. Finally, you must agree to the terms, and then click the button to submit the theme for approval.

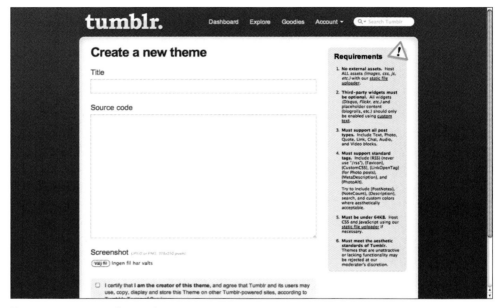

FIGURE 10-23: The submit a theme page

When you have themes submitted, you can manage them from the Manage your themes page at `http://www.tumblr.com/themes/manage`. From there you can also easily reach the page for submitting a new theme.

Hosting Your Theme Outside the Theme Garden

If you don't want or are unable to host your theme at Tumblr's Theme Garden, you can always host it yourself. All you need is someplace to put a file containing your theme content where others can access it. This could be a Web host using FTP, or on SourceForge (`http://sourceforge.net`) or Github (`https://github.com`), assuming you meet the requirements of these services. Another solution would be to use a public folder with a service such as Dropbox (`http://dropbox.com`).

Hosting your theme outside of the Theme Garden comes with some issues, however. The most obvious concerns are how people are to find it and whether you want to offer it for use free of charge. Most Tumblr users go to the Theme Garden and pick a theme, but they won't find self-hosted themes there. Instead you'll have to rely on search engines, links, and word of mouth to spread your theme.

The theme code is the easy part. Just offer a file as a download and instruct the user to copy and paste its content into the Custom HTML box. However, images are a problem because they will have to be uploaded to Tumblr using the static file uploader. Either that, or you'll have to host them externally.

Want to Sell Your Theme?

So you created an awesome Tumblr theme that you think people would want to pay money for. The obvious choice would be to sell it on Tumblr's Theme Garden, but it isn't that easy. In fact, the only ways to get on the premium theme bandwagon within the Theme Garden are to be invited or to contact Tumblr and ask nicely. There are no public details as to the deal between Tumblr and the theme designers, so we're all in the dark here.

If the Theme Garden is off limits to you, there are some third-party marketplaces you might want to check out:

- ThemeForest: `http://themeforest.net/category/blogging/tumblr`
- Obox: `http://www.obox-design.com/tumblr-themes.cfm`
- Mojo Themes: `http://www.mojo-themes.com/categories/tumblr/`

These sites are a lot more lenient when it comes to allowing you to sell your theme. But then again, they are not Tumblr so finding customers and getting sales here will be harder than on the Theme Garden.

The marketplaces listed here are operated by individual companies. You should definitely research any third-party marketplace before submitting a theme for reselling. **NOTE**

Another option is to sell the theme yourself, from your own site, charging for it using PayPal or some other solution. Marketplaces will probably result in more sales and exposure, though, so consider your business model carefully when it comes to Tumblr themes. Good luck!

Summary

With the knowledge you've gained from Chapters 9 and 10, you now know enough to edit the themes available on Tumblr as well as create your own. You can use your newfound knowledge to make the most of your Tumblr sites, making them fit your needs and your ideas.

Tumblr is a truly powerful publishing platform offering loads of possibilities. The fact that it is so easy to use is its greatest strength. Combine that with the social aspects of the service and you have a platform that can work for you in so many ways.

I'm sure you'll be able to create amazing things with Tumblr. And since you've finished this book, I'm more than confident that you'll be able to tackle any potential problems along the way.

Now go publish something!

appendix A

Using HTML and CSS with Tumblr

in this appendix

- Learn the do's and don'ts of HTML and CSS
- Find great resources to learn more

THIS APPENDIX OFFERS some tips on writing HTML and CSS, the most important markup languages of the Web. It is not a guide to writing HTML or CSS, but reinforces some best practices that will improve your coding for Tumblr themes.

Do's and Don'ts of HTML and CSS

This is not a book about how to write HTML and CSS (although you can find a list of dedicated resources on that topic at the end of this appendix). However, as both HTML and CSS are integral parts of Tumblr themes, I want to remind you of some common practices that you should observe when working in Tumblr themes:

- Make sure that your code validates. You can check for yourself at http://validator.w3.org.

- Use tags the way they are meant to be used. In other words, don't use the h1 heading to format footnotes; that's not the purpose of the tag.

- Use the heading tags. You have h1 through h6 tags at your disposal, and while it might be easier to just bold text into a heading, you should avoid doing that. Search engines and accessibility software rely on h1, h2, h3, and if that's not a good enough reason for you, it is just plain right to use the tags at your disposal.

- Don't div out. Placing several div containers around everything is sometimes necessary to achieve the layout you're after, but don't overuse the div tag if you don't need to. Keep it simple and take the time to figure out how you can best achieve your layout.

- Close all HTML tags. Sure, you don't need to close the p or li tags for them to work, but it is considered bad practice not to, and it is bound to get you in trouble sooner or later.

- Use lowercase for tags. Although you are allowed to use uppercase for tags if you like, most people agree that lowercase is friendlier to the eye.

- Use unordered lists for menus. The ul tag is for lists, and what is a menu if not a list of items? It is semantically correct, so remember this, and apply the principle to other elements of your site as well.

- Keep the HTML markup as clean as possible, moving every design element to your CSS. This gives you a lot more control and makes the code a lot easier to read and maintain.

- Don't write inline style. You can put CSS within the actual HTML tags, overriding everything, but that isn't a good idea. You're better off isolating your CSS to the style tag in the head section of your document. In fact, you should keep your CSS in a separate file, including it in the head section, but this doesn't work well with Tumblr theming since most themes consist of one single file.

- Remember: In CSS, IDs can only be used once per page, whereas classes can be used over and over again.

- Name your code elements appropriately. If your CSS class is for a side column, name it `side-column`. This makes the code a lot easier to read and edit later on.

- Leave comments in the code. If you have solutions that might be hard to grasp, or remember for that matter, add inline comments as a reminder for you or whoever might be reading the code.

- Split the CSS into sections. The more advanced your design, the more CSS you'll write. It is usually a good idea to create sections of various types of styles, like links, typography, and so on, using inline comments to show the reader where a section starts.

- Consider loading JavaScript libraries last. That means that the JavaScript code won't load until the rest of the page has loaded; you most likely won't need it until then anyway.

- Avoid inline JavaScript; it is a lot better to load external resources.

- Use the alt attribute with images. This practice is important for image description, for accessibility reasons, and those who browse the Web in text-only mode.

- Question every graphic. Sometimes you could achieve the same effect with CSS, which is almost always a better option.

- Test in all modern browsers. There are quite a few, from Internet Explorer, Firefox, and Safari to Google Chrome, Opera and the full slew of mobile web browsers out there. Test as much as you can; unfortunately not all browsers interpret even perfect code perfectly.

HTML and CSS Resources

There are a plethora of books and websites available to help you learn the fine art of HTML and CSS, the markup languages of the web. The resources listed here will get you started if you are new to these coding languages, or provide a nice refresher course if your knowledge has gotten a bit rusty.

Books

A quick search on Amazon will turn up dozens of books on HTML and CSS. Here are a few recommendations.

- *Beginning HTML, XHTML, CSS, and JavaScript* (Wrox, 2009) by Jon Duckett

- *Beginning HTML, XHTML, CSS, and JavaScript*, 5th Edition (Wrox, 2010) by Steven M. Schafer

- *Learn HTML and CSS with w3Schools* (Wiley 2010) by w3Schools

- *Teach Yourself VISUALLY HTML and CSS* (Wiley 2008) by Mike Wooldridge and Linda Wooldridge

- *HTML, XHTML and CSS For Dummies, 7th Edition* (Wiley, 2011) by Ed Tittel and Jeff Noble

Online Resources

There are quite a few options online when it comes to learning HTML and CSS. The following list shows a select few that I recommend for learning the basics. You'll no doubt find more if you turn to your favorite search engine and start looking for tutorials and how-tos.

- **W3** (`http://w3.org`) is the home of the specifications and a good technical reference.

- **w3Schools** (`http://w3schools.com`) has great tutorials for both HTML and CSS.

- **HTMLGoodies** (`http://www.htmlgoodies.com`) is an oldie but goodie when it comes to learning HTML in particular.

- **Tizag** (`http://www.tizag.com`) is another good tutorial site that will help you with HTML and CSS.

- **CSSPlay** (`http://www.cssplay.co.uk`) teaches CSS.

Index